THE ULTIMATE
MIAMI DOLPHINS
TRIVIA BOOK

A Collection of Amazing Trivia Quizzes
and Fun Facts for Die-Hard Dolphins Fans!

Ray Walker

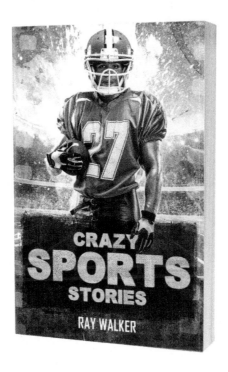

CONTENTS

INTRODUCTION

The Miami Dolphins joined the American Football League at a time of great growth for the league. Their four years in the AFL wasn't a great time for the Dolphins, but those experiences laid the groundwork for a quick start once the AFL and NFL merged in 1970. Three straight Super Bowl appearances from 1971 through 1973 set the table for three decades of success in South Florida as the Dolphins evolved and matured. It's been much harder for the franchise over the last two decades, but things are looking up again for the oldest professional sports franchise in Florida as it heads into the third decade of the 21st century.

This book will cover all the eras in Dolphins lore, from those struggles in the AFL to the Super Bowl victories of the early 1970s and the playoff successes in the 1980s and 1990s. We'll quiz you on all of your favorite players and coaches over the next 12 chapters, which are full of fun facts and interesting nuggets about the Miami Dolphins and their history. The goal is for you to finish this book knowing much more about your favorite NFL franchise than when you took it off your shelf.

This book is designed to test the most die-hard Dolphins fans with trivia that will keep you on the edge of your seat. Each of the chapters in this book focuses on a specific topic, from the history of the franchise to specific positions and the record book. In each chapter, there is a mix of 20 multiple-choice and true-or-false questions, followed by the answers to those questions (on a separate page) and 10 fun "Did You Know" facts that offer some behind-the-scenes information about the Dolphins. Please do not be alarmed if some of these questions stump you; the whole point of the book is to help you learn more about your favorite team, so don't expect to ace every chapter.

We want you to learn something new by devouring this book so that you can use your newfound knowledge to show off to your fellow Dolphins fans. All of the information conveyed in this book is current as of the end of the 2020 season. All you need to do now is sit back, relax, and enjoy the hours of fun this book provides for the biggest Miami Dolphins fans in the world.

CHAPTER 1:

ORIGINS & HISTORY

QUIZ TIME!

1. Which famous television star was a part-owner with Joe Robbie when the AFL awarded a franchise to Miami in 1965?

   a. Bob Hope
   b. Danny Thomas
   c. Andy Griffith
   d. Dick Van Dyke

2. In which state did Joe Robbie run for governor in 1950?

   a. Minnesota
   b. Florida
   c. North Dakota
   d. South Dakota

3. Who was the first coach of the Miami Dolphins?

   a. Don Shula
   b. Joe Robbie
   c. George Wilson
   d. John Madden

4. Don Shula coached the Dolphins in their final AFL season.

   a. True

   b. False

5. How many straight losses did the Dolphins suffer in their inaugural season before finally beating Denver for the franchise's first victory?

   a. 4

   b. 5

   c. 6

   d. 7

6. Which team was the first NFL team the Dolphins defeated?

   a. Philadelphia Eagles

   b. Atlanta Falcons

   c. Washington Redskins

   d. Dallas Cowboys

7. When was the first season the Dolphins had a losing record in the NFL?

   a. 1970

   b. 1974

   c. 1975

   d. 1976

8. The Dolphins lost their season opener in 1973, one year after completing the only perfect season in NFL history.

   a. True

   b. False

9. In which year did the Dolphins move from the Orange Bowl to Joe Robbie Stadium?

    a. 1985
    b. 1986
    c. 198
    d. 1988

10. Which of these celebrities has not bought a small ownership share in the Dolphins from Stephen Ross?

    a. Jimmy Buffett
    b. Gloria Estefan
    c. Serena Williams
    d. Fergie

11. What did Joe Auer do with the opening kickoff of Miami's first-ever regular-season game against Oakland?

    a. He fumbled.
    b. He scored on a 95-yard return.
    c. The play resulted in a safety.
    d. He recovered an onside kick.

12. Who caught the Dolphins' first postseason touchdown pass in their 21-14 loss to Oakland?

    a. Paul Warfield
    b. Jim Kiick
    c. Larry Csonka
    d. Bob Griese

13. Dan Marino was the first Dolphins quarterback to throw for 2,500 yards in a season.

a. True

b. False

14. Who was the first member of the Dolphins to be elected to the Pro Football Hall of Fame?

a. Larry Csonka

b. Jim Langer

c. Brian Griese

d. Paul Warfield

15. Which famous college coach finished an unremarkable 15-17 in two seasons as Miami's head coach?

a. Nick Saban

b. Bear Bryant

c. Steve Spurrier

d. Bobby Bowden

16. How many times has Miami won its division since moving to the NFL in 1970?

a. 13

b. 14

c. 15

d. 16

17. Who was the last coach to lead the Dolphins to the playoffs?

a. Adam Gase

b. Tony Sporano

c. Dave Wannstedt

d. Don Shula

18. Who was the last team Miami beat in the playoffs?

    a. Baltimore Ravens
    b. Seattle Seahawks
    c. Indianapolis Colts
    d. Buffalo Bills

19. Matt Moore threw the last touchdown pass in Miami's playoff history.

    a. Tru
    b. False

20. In which season did Don Shula surpass George Halas' record for most wins as an NFL head coach?

    a. 1990
    b. 1991
    c. 1992
    d. 1993

QUIZ ANSWERS

1. B – Danny Thomas

2. D – South Dakota

3. C – George Wilson

4. B – False

5. B – 5

6. A – Philadelphia Eagles

7. D – 1976

8. B – False

9. C – 1987

10. Trick question; all of them own a minority share in the team.

11. B – He scored on a 95-yard return.

12. A – Paul Warfield

13. A – True

14. D – Paul Warfield

15. A — Nick Saban

16. B – 14

17. A – Adam Gase

18. C – Indianapolis Colts

19. A – True

20. D – 1993

DID YOU KNOW?

1. Miami almost got an AFL franchise when the league first opened for business in 1960. Ralph Wilson Jr., who at the time was a minority owner in the NFL's Detroit Lions, actually approached Miami in 1959 about securing a deal to use the Orange Bowl for home games. The two sides never reached an agreement, so Wilson took his franchise to Buffalo and the Bills became a charter member of the new league instead.

2. Joe Robbie was hired by an ownership group in Philadelphia to try to lure the AFL to their city when they learned that Robbie was a college friend of AFL Commissioner Joe Foss. It was Foss who told Robbie that the league was looking to add a team in the south and not compete with the NFL in Philadelphia. When the ownership group in Philly passed on the option of purchasing the team in Miami, Robbie stepped in to actually purchase the Dolphins along with actor Danny Thomas.

3. Danny Thomas is probably best known for his efforts to build and fund St. Jude Children's Research Hospital in Tennessee but those efforts led to him becoming part of the original ownership group. Thomas and Robbie are both Lebanese-American and Thomas used every connection he had in that community to help raise funds

for the hospital. Robbie was a member of the executive committee and worked as a budget director on the project, and he hosted a reception to help Thomas raise the money. When Robbie then learned the AFL was looking to expand into Miami in 1965, he called upon his connections with Thomas and helped find the group that would raise the $7.5 million to buy the franchise.

4. The Dolphins' nickname came out of a public contest to name the team in conjunction with the local media. The contest drew almost 20,000 entries and more than 600 of them chose the "Dolphins" as the team's new name. Robbie explained the choice by telling the crowd on the day of the announcement: "The dolphin is one of the fastest and smartest creatures of the sea. Dolphins can attack and kill a shark or a whale. Sailors say bad luck will come to anyone who harms one of them."

5. For their first three seasons in the AFL, the Dolphins had a live dolphin in a tank on the east end of the Orange Bowl. The mascot was named Flipper, and they would celebrate touchdowns and field goals by jumping in the tank. Robbie struck a deal with the city and the Seaquarium to transport a dolphin to and from the stadium every Sunday. The tank was removed in 1968 because the city and Seaquarium refused to pay for the repairs to the tank and take on the cost of transporting the dolphin to home games. The Dolphins introduced a traditional dolphin mascot named T.D. in 1997.

6. You can thank the local newspaper for the Dolphins hiring Don Shula to be the team's head coach in 1970. When Robbie was looking for a new coach after firing George Wilson, he was chatting with *Miami Herald* sports editor Edwin Pope and beat writer Bill Braucher about the situation. Someone mentioned Shula's name, and Robbie said "That's the guy." Braucher and Shula knew each other from their time at John Carroll University and it was Pope and Braucher who set up the initial contact between Shula and Robbie. One 1971 first-round pick to the Baltimore Colts later and the Dolphins had their legendary coach.

7. Robbie's decision to build his own stadium in Miami Gardens was widely criticized. Yet Robbie somehow convinced owners to vote for the Super Bowl to be played at his new unbuilt and unfinanced stadium in 1989. He used the 10-year contracts on club seats and sold luxury suites in the new stadium to show the banks he had the income to pay off his loans, then sold his soccer team and private plane to help break ground on the new stadium. The stadium itself got off to an inauspicious start because its opening coincided with the NFL player strike, meaning the first scheduled regular-season game for Joe Robbie Stadium was postponed and the actual first game was played with scrubs.

8. The Dolphins lost their first nine games as a franchise, four preseason games followed by the first five regular-season games in team history. Miami's first preseason game was on August 6, 1966, against the San Diego Chargers in San

Diego and their first home game was the following week, a 33-0 loss to Kansas City Chiefs. The regular season wasn't much better, as the Dolphins lost to Oakland, the Jets, Buffalo, San Diego, and Oakland again before their 24-7 win over Denver at home. The Dolphins even went on their first winning streak by beating Houston on the road the following week. Miami lost six straight games and then ended its inaugural season with a 29-28 win over Houston.

9. From 1970 to 71, Larry King (yes, that Larry King from CNN and his many other talk shows after he left the network) was a color analyst for the Miami Dolphins radio broadcast. He was doing a talk show on WIOD in Miami at the time and the network decided he would be a good second color commentator in the radio booth alongside Henry Barrow. The agreement only lasted two seasons, however, after one of King's former business partners accused King of grand larceny and the station fired King, though the charges were later dropped.

10. After Stephen Ross purchased 95 percent of the Dolphins from Wayne Huizenga in 2009, he began selling off small shares to many different celebrities. Among the famous people who purchased part of the team were Jennifer Lopez, Marc Antony, Fergie, Serena and Venus Williams, and Gloria Estefan. In a *USA Today* story about the new celebrity owners, Ross told the newspaper, "We've eliminated the exclusivity of it being an all-white man's club. That's what I want people to feel. We want you."

CHAPTER 2:

NUMBERS GAME

QUIZ TIME!

1. How many numbers have the Dolphins officially retired?

    a. 2
    b. 3
    c. 4
    d. 5

2. Who was the only person to wear the No. 13 for the Dolphins before Dan Marino's arrival in Miami?

    a. Jake Scott
    b. Dick Wood
    c. George Wilson Jr.
    d. Earl Morrall

3. Which of these specialists did not wear No. 1 for the Dolphins?

    a. Matt Turk
    b. Cody Parkey
    c. Joe Nedney
    d. Garo Yepremian

4. The first player to wear No. 14 for the Dolphins was a replacement player during the 1987 players' strike.

   a. True
   b. False

5. What number did Miami's first-round pick in the 1966 AFL Draft, Rick Norton, wear during his tenure with the team?

   a. 3
   b. 4
   c. 7
   d. 11

6. Mercury Morris made the No. 22 famous in Miami, but which of these running backs also wore 22 for the Dolphins?

   a. Frank Gore
   b. Ronnie Brown
   c. Reggie Bush
   d. Knowshon Moreno

7. Which of these players was not the first person to wear his uniform number in Dolphins history?

   a. Bob Matheson, 53
   b. Jim Langer, 62
   c. Larry Little, 66
   d. Bob Kuechenberg, 67

8. Larry Csonka's No. 39 is the only Dolphin uniform number to be worn by only one player in the team's history.

a. True

b. False

9. Which single-digit number was the last to make its debut on a Dolphins player?

    a. 5

    b. 6

    c. 8

    d. 9

10. Which number did Olindo Mare wear for his 10 seasons as the kicker for the Dolphins?

    a. 9

    b. 10

    c. 11

    d. 17

11. O.J. McDuffie tortured secondaries in the AFC for eight seasons in the No. 81 for the Dolphins. Who succeeded him as the wearer of that number after he was forced to retire in 2001?

    a. Marty Booker

    b. James McKnight

    c. Chris Chambers

    d. Randy McMichael

12. Which number did Dick Wood wear when he was the Miami Dolphins' first starting quarterback?

    a. 15

    b. 16

c. 17

d. 18

13. No one has worn No. 54 or 99 for Miami since Zach Thomas and Jason Taylor retired from the team in 2007 and 2011, respectively.

    a. True

    b. False

14. Which number was not worn by a Dolphins player who is enshrined in the Hall of Fame?

    a. 34

    b. 57

    c. 63

    d. 42

15. Which number did future NFL coach Doug Pederson wear during his one season as Dan Marino's backup in Miami?

    a. 10

    b. 11

    c. 12

    d. 14

16. Which number did Larry Seiple wear when he was setting the record for the most punts in Miami Dolphins history?

    a. 0

    b. 10

    c. 20

    d. 30

17. The Dolphins have had someone wear every official number between 1 and 99.

    a. True
    b. False

18. What is the official name of the Dolphins' greenish primary color?

    a. Aqua
    b. Sea green
    c. Marsh green
    d. Dolphin green

19. The helmet on the dolphin in the Dolphins main logo was introduced in 1974 during the first major redesign of the logo.

    a. True
    b. False

20. Which was the first season during which the Dolphins wore an orange jersey for at least one game?

    a. 1993
    b. 1998
    c. 2000
    d. 2003

QUIZ ANSWERS

1. B – 3

2. A – Jake Scott

3. C – Joe Nedney

4. A – True

5. D – 11

6. C – Reggie Bush

7. A – Bob Matheson

8. B – False

9. C – 8

10. B – 10

11. D – Randy McMichael

12. D – 18

13. B – False

14. C – 63

15. D – 14

16. C – 20

17. A – True

18. A – Aqua

19. B – False

20. D – 2003

DID YOU KNOW?

1. The Dolphins' primary colors have not really changed since the franchise's founding in 1966. The aqua and orange combination has been the staple of Miami's professional football team and have featured prominently on every uniform in the team's history. Michael MacCambridge told NFL.com once that he felt there was a strong connection between Miami and the Dolphins' uniform colors that most cities do not have. "The colors of the Dolphins perfectly evoke the City of Miami. The colors do depict the area. This is how we dress; we wear these colors. Our houses are these colors; there are a lot of pink houses, blue houses. We don't have dark colors in Miami."

2. The Miami Dolphins were very quick to retire Bob Griese's No. 12, doing so in May 1982, just two years after he retired from the league. It didn't take even that long for the Dolphins to honor Dan Marino, as his No. 13 was retired at halftime of Miami's second home game of the 2000 season, right after Marino retired in 1999. It did take much longer for Larry Csonka to receive his due as the Dolphins officially retired No. 39 in December 2002, after the number had been unofficially retired for nearly 25 years after Csonka last played for the Dolphins.

3. The art of unofficially retiring a number is normally left up to the equipment manager. In Miami's case, there were

three who upheld the tradition for Csonka. It began with Dan Dowe, who refused to issue the No. 39 to anyone after Csonka bolted for the World Football League and then again when he left the Dolphins in 1979. When Dowe left the team, Bobby Monica kept the tradition going after interning with Dowe before taking over the job full-time. Then Tony Egues replaced Monica and the moratorium on players wearing No. 39 continued until the Dolphins finally retired it in 2002.

4. No. 13 for the Miami Dolphins will always belong to Marino, but the manner in which he acquired the number is quite interesting. Marino's father was his youth football coach, so it seemed only fair that he get the last choice of jersey numbers. The No. 13 was in the pile, so Marino grabbed it and he never changed through high school, college, or the pros. The number is retired in his honor at the University of Pittsburgh and with the Dolphins, giving him a lasting legacy to a traditionally unlucky number.

5. It would have also made sense if the Dolphins had retired the No. 13 before Marino even arrived in Miami. Jake Scott was the MVP of Super Bowl VII, which capped off the Dolphins' undefeated season in 1972 by intercepting two passes in Miami's win. He intercepted 35 passes in his six seasons with the team, which still stands as the franchise's career record. Scott was named to the Pro Bowl every year from 1971 through 1975 until he defected to the World Football League in search of more money.

6. When Jason Taylor was traded from Miami to Washington in 2008, many assumed he would take the No. 99 with him. Even Andre Carter, who was wearing No. 99 for the Redskins at the time, believed that Taylor would ask for the number when he arrived. Instead, Taylor decided on wearing No. 55, telling the media after his first practice, "I talked to my wife and decided we'd let 99 stay in Miami and start a new chapter up here." He returned to wearing No. 99 in his final two stints with the Dolphins as well as in his one season with the Jets in 2010.

7. Olindo Mare wore No. 10 during his 10 seasons with the Dolphins. He inherited the number from his predecessor, Pete Stoyanovich. Mare attended a Dolphins practice and saw Stoyanovich wearing the No. 10 and connected it with the great No. 10s who have played soccer. As he told the *Sun Sentinel* in 1999, "I saw he was wearing No. 10. That's the magic number in soccer. It's the number all the great players wear. When I saw him wearing No. 10, it means you're the best, and so when I saw him wearing that, I thought maybe I could do what he had done."

8. The single-digit numbers have not been very popular in Dolphin history. Only the No. 7 has been worn by at least 10 different players over the last 50-plus years. Only four players have worn the No. 1 entering the 2020 season, four have donned No. 2, eight have worn No. 3, five have played in No. 4, eight have been in No. 5, seven in No. 6, four have donned No. 8, and six have worn No. 9.

9. When Tua Tagovailoa took the field for the Dolphins in 2020 wearing No. 1, he became the first non-specialist to wear the number for Miami. Tagovailoa wore No. 13 in college and many thought Marino might allow the Dolphins' first-round pick to wear the number, but Tagovailoa declined and instead chose to wear No. 1. The number was made most famous by Garo Yepremian, who was the kicker for the Dolphins during their glory days in the 1970s.

10. In a CBS Sports column from July 2020, eight players with ties to the Dolphins were named the greatest player to ever wear their number. Csonka and Marino both represented their numbers for the Dolphins, as did longtime offensive linemen Jim Langer (62), Larry Little (66), and Bob Kuechenberg (67). Three others made short pitstops in Miami during their careers: Jay Cutler (6), Troy Vincent (23), and Junior Seau (55).

CHAPTER 3:

CALLING THE SIGNALS

QUIZ TIME!

1. How many regular-season games did Dan Marino win for the Dolphins?

    a. 136

    b. 142

    c. 147

    d. 153

2. Which quarterback has the most wins while still having a losing record as a starter for the Dolphins?

    a. Jay Cutler

    b. Chad Henne

    c. Jay Fiedler

    d. Ryan Tannehill

3. John Stofa is the only quarterback in Dolphins history to win all of his starts for Miami.

    a. True

    b. False

4. Which of these quarterbacks won more than one game as the Dolphins starting quarterback?

    a. Trent Green
    b. Cleo Lemon
    c. Brock Osweiler
    d. Daunte Culpepper

5. Which of these quarterbacks never threw for 400 yards in a game for Miami?

    a. Chad Pennington
    b. Chad Henne
    c. Joey Harrington
    d. Don Strock

6. Who holds the Dolphins record for most consecutive pass completions?

    a. Chad Pennington
    b. Dan Marino
    c. Bob Griese
    d. Ryan Tannehill

7. Jay Fiedler holds the record for how many consecutive games without throwing an interception?

    a. 4
    b. 5
    c. 6
    d. 7

8. No Dolphins quarterback other than Dan Marino has thrown 30 or more touchdown passes in a season.

a. True

b. False

9. Who threw the longest pass in Dolphin history?

    a. Dan Marino

    b. Chad Henne

    c. Bob Griese

    d. Jay Fiedler

10. How many times has a Dolphins quarterback completed two-thirds of his passes in a season (minimum 75 completions)?

    a. 1

    b. 2

    c. 4

    d. 5

11. In which season did Dan Marino set the Dolphins record for most passing yards in a season?

    a. 1984

    b. 1986

    c. 1988

    d. 1994

12. How many of the top-10 single-game passing yard totals belong to Dan Marino?

    a. 7

    b. 8

    c. 9

    d. 10

13. How many times did Dan Marino lead the NFL in passing yards?

    a. 2

    b. 3

    c. 4

    d. 5

14. Dan Marino set the mark for most passing yards in a game in the same game in which he tied Bob Griese's franchise record with 6 touchdown passes.

    a. True

    b. False

15. Which of the following statements about Dan Marino's career with Miami is false?

    a. More passing yards than the quarterbacks ranked second through fourth combined

    b. More 300-yard passing games than all other Dolphins quarterbacks combined

    c. More than a third of all the completed passes in team history

    d. More than a quarter of the interceptions thrown in team history

16. How many games did Bob Griese start for the Miami Dolphins?

    a. 152

    b. 157

    c. 161

    d. 168

17. What was Bob Griese's career high for passing yards in a season?

    a. 2,473
    b. 2,567
    c. 2,645
    d. 2,719

18. How many touchdowns did Bob Griese throw in 1977, when he led the NFL in passing touchdowns for the only time in his career?

    a. 19
    b. 20
    c. 21
    d. 22

19. Who was not one of the opponents for Bob Griese's three 300-yard games with the Dolphins?

    a. Houston Oilers
    b. Cincinnati Bengals
    c. New York Jets
    d. Kansas City Chiefs

20. No quarterback other than Bob Griese and Dan Marino has thrown t touchdown passes in a game.

    a. True
    b. False

QUIZ ANSWERS

1. C – 147

2. D – Ryan Tannehill

3. B – False

4. C – Brock Osweiler

5. A – Chad Pennington

6. D – Ryan Tannehill

7. B – 5

8. A – True

9. C – Bob Griese

10. B – 2

11. A – 1984

12. C – 9

13. D – 5

14. B – False

15. C – Accounts for more than a third of all the completed passes in team history

16. A – 152

17. A – 2,473

18. D – 22

19. C – New York Jets

20. A – True

DID YOU KNOW?

1. Even though it took six weeks for Dan Marino to start his first NFL game in 1983, it didn't take nearly that long for coach Don Shula to know Marino was the better quarterback. David Woodley had led the Dolphins to the Super Bowl in 1982 and earned the starting job, but Shula said he could tell in the spring after drafting Marino the difference in the two quarterbacks. "When we got them together for the first time on the field and had Woodley throwing on one side to a group of receivers and Marino on the other, it was so evident the ability Dan had throwing the football. Woodley was an athlete playing quarterback and Marino was a quarterback playing quarterback. You could just look at it and see, even in the simplest passing drills, that Marino had that great skill."

2. Before Bob Griese was elected to the Pro Football Hall of Fame, a part of his gameday attire was already enshrined in Canton. In 1978, 12 years before his induction, Griese donated the glasses he wore during games to the Hall of Fame for display. Griese became one of the first players to wear glasses during play because he was legally blind in one of his eyes. In an episode of *Peyton's Place* on ESPN+, Griese said the condition went undiscovered in school because he would cheat on the vision exams when it came time to test his bad eye.

3. Bob wasn't the only Griese to play for the Dolphins. His son, Brian, started five games for Miami and won three of them in 2003. Brian spent one season in Miami, throwing for 813 yards, 5 touchdowns, and 6 interceptions while completing 56.9 percent of his passes. Before joining the Dolphins, Griese won the 1998 Super Bowl as John Elway's backup in Denver, so Brian and Bob became the first father-son duo to both win the Super Bowl.

4. Earl Morrall was the quintessential backup quarterback, having served as the primary backup behind five Hall-of-Famers. Most Dolphins fans will know him from his season-saving play in 1972 after Bob Griese went down with an injury. Morrall came in to lead Miami to a win over San Diego when Griese got hurt and then won nine straight games as a starter to lead the Dolphins to a perfect regular season. He then won two playoff games as a starter, though he was replaced in the AFC Championship Game by Griese. In fact, almost all Morrall did in Miami was win as he finished with a 13-1 record in 14 starts over five seasons as Griese's backup.

5. Jay Fiedler's road to Miami was arduous for the five-year Dolphins starter. The quarterback left Dartmouth with school records in career touchdown passes, passing yards, and total offense, giving him a glimmer of hope for the NFL. He spent two seasons as the third-string quarterback in Philadelphia as an undrafted free agent and then played in NFL Europe in 1997 after not being invited to an NFL training camp. He sent videos to every NFL team after that

season in Europe. Only the Minnesota Vikings responded and they signed him. He played in five games for Minnesota before getting his first start in 1999 for Jacksonville. The 317 yards he threw for in a Week 17 win over Cincinnati was enough to convince the Dolphins to sign him and he went 36-23 as Miami's starter over the next five years.

6. Chad Pennington is the only player ever to be named the Associated Press NFL Comeback Player of the Year twice, doing so in 2006 with the Jets and then again two years later with Miami. Pennington led the Dolphins to an 11-5 record and the AFC East division title in his first season with the franchise in 2008. He led the league with a 67.4 percent completion percentage that year while throwing for a career-best 3,653 yards. He threw 19 touchdowns compared to just 7 interceptions in rallying Miami to nine wins in its last 10 games to storm into the playoffs with momentum. The magic ran out for Pennington in the playoffs, however, as he threw 4 interceptions in a wild card round loss to Baltimore to close out the year.

7. Ryan Tannehill had a very unique career in Miami. He started the third-most games in franchise history and his 42 wins as a starter is the third most in team history, but he's just one of two quarterbacks with at least 10 wins for the Dolphins who had a losing record as a starter. His overall record of 42-46 caused Miami to cut ties with him after seven years as the starter in 2018, only for Tannehill to turn around his career after leaving the Dolphins.

8. Only seven quarterbacks have started playoff games for the Dolphins in their history with a combined record of 20-21. Marino won 8 of his 18 postseason starts and Bob Griese went 6-5 in the playoffs. Woodley was 3-2, Fiedler went 1-2, Morrall won both of his starts, and Chad Pennington and Matt Moore each lost his only playoff start for Miami.

9. The Dolphins have had seven quarterbacks lose all of their starts for the team in their career and only two who won all of them. George Mira won his only start for the Dolphins in 1971 and John Stofa won both of his starts for Miami, one in 1966 and one in 1967. Among the winless starters, only Tyler Thigpen had just one start for Miami. Trent Green lost all five of his starts for Miami in 2007, John Beck and Dick Wood both lost four starts, Josh Rosen lost all three of his starts, and Bernie Kosar and Sage Rosenfels each lost twice.

10. Mira did not last long in his one start and didn't do anything to help Miami win. He was starting against the Pittsburgh Steelers that day because Bob Griese had been hospitalized the day before the game with stomach issues. Mira misfired on both of his passing attempts in the game and the Dolphin offense barely moved, allowing the Steelers to take a 14-3 lead. Griese entered the game at the end of the first quarter and led the Dolphins to 21 unanswered points after fumbling away his first snap for a 24-21 victory.

CHAPTER 4:

BETWEEN THE TACKLES

QUIZ TIME!

1. Who is the only Dolphins running back to lead the NFL in rushing for a season?

   a. Larry Csonka
   b. Ronnie Brown
   c. Ricky Williams
   d. Mercury Morris

2. How many times has a Dolphins running back run for 200 yards in a game?

   a. 5
   b. 7
   c. 9
   d. 11

3. How many times did Ricky Williams run for 100 yards in a game to set Miami's career record?

   a. 24
   b. 22

c. 19

d. 16

4. How long was Lamar Miller's record-setting touchdown run in 2014 against the New York Jets?

    a. 85 yards

    b. 89 yards

    c. 93 yards

    d. 97 yards

5. Karim Abdul-Jabbar holds the Dolphins rookie record for rushing yards in a game.

    a. True

    b. False

6. Which of these running backs does not share the team record with rushing touchdowns in five consecutive games?

    a. Pete Johnson

    b. Mercury Morris

    c. Don Nottingham

    d. Ronnie Brown

7. Who was the opponent when Ronnie Brown set the single-game record for most rushing touchdowns in a game?

    a. Buffalo Bills

    b. New York Jets

    c. New England Patriots

    d. Indianapolis Colts

8. Dolphins backs have rushed for 1,000 yards 14 times.

    a. True
    b. False

9. Who was the last Dolphins running back to lead the NFL in rushing touchdowns?

    a. Mercury Morris
    b. Karim Abdul-Jabbar
    c. Ricky Williams
    d. Lamar Smith

10. How many yards separate the first- and second-place rushers on Miami's career rushing list?

    a. 301
    b. 458
    c. 523
    d. 697

11. What was the longest run of Larry Csonka's career?

    a. 49 yards
    b. 51 yards
    c. 54 yards
    d. 59 yards

12. How many touchdowns did Larry Csonka score during the 1973 playoff run that ended with him being named the Super Bowl MVP?

    a. 4
    b. 5
    c. 6
    d. 7

13. Larry Csonka was Miami's leading rusher when he returned to the Dolphins to finish his career in 1979.

    a. True
    b. False

14. What is Mercury Morris' given first name?

    a. Edward
    b. Michael
    c. Eugene
    d. Mercury

15. What was the only season in which Mercury Morris led the Dolphins in rushing?

    a. 1972
    b. 1973
    c. 1974
    d. 1975

16. How many of the top five rushers in Dolphin history were teammates with each other in the early 1970s?

    a. 2
    b. 3
    c. 4
    d. 5

17. How many rushing touchdowns did Karim Abdul-Jabbar have during his record-breaking rookie year for the Dolphins in 1996?

    a. 9
    b. 12

c. 10

d. 11

18. Who was the last Dolphins player to rush for 10 touchdowns in a season?

a. Ricky Williams

b. Ronnie Brown

c. Lamar Miller

d. Jay Ajayi

19. Which of these running backs with 1,000-yard seasons in Miami did the Dolphins draft?

a. Reggie Bush

b. Lamar Miller

c. Lamar Smith

d. Delvin Williams

20. Ryan Fitzpatrick became the first person to lead the Dolphins in rushing with less than 300 yards when he ran for 243 yards to lead the team in 2019.

a. True

b. False

QUIZ ANSWERS

1. C – Ricky Williams

2. B – 7

3. A – 24

4. D – 97 yards

5. B – False

6. D – Ronnie Brown

7. C – New England Patriots

8. A – True

9. B – Karim Abdul-Jabbar

10. A – 301

11. C – 54 yards

12. C – 6

13. A – True

14. C – Eugene

15. D – 1975

16. B – 3

17. D – 11

18. A – Ricky Williams

19. B – Lamar Miller

20. B – False

DID YOU KNOW?

1. Joe Auer will forever be known as the first person to score a touchdown in Miami Dolphins history. The running back caught the opening kickoff at his own 5-yard line and some excellent blocking carved a hole in the middle of the field for him. Around his own 40-yard line, he cut to his left, switched the ball to his left arm, and took off. He was nearly tripped up at the Raiders' 5-yard line, but he stumbled into the end zone for the first points of the Dolphins franchise. Auer ended the season by being named the team's MVP after rushing for 416 yards and 4 touchdowns and adding 22 catches for 263 yards and another 4 touchdowns.

2. The duo of Jim Kiick and Larry Csonka was nicknamed Butch Cassidy and the Sundance Kid after the bank robbers from the 1969 movie of the same name. The two were roommates and drinking buddies throughout their career and were two-thirds of the terrifying trio of running backs that made the Dolphins of the 1970s so difficult to defend. The two wrote a book together in 1974 along with *New York Times* columnist Dave Anderson, *Always on the Run,* about their life in the NFL and their journey to the league.

3. Csonka and Kiick were also two of the three Dolphins who left the team after the 1974 season due to contract issues.

The duo and receiver Paul Warfield all signed with the Memphis Southmen of the World Football League on a three-year guaranteed contract. However, after the league folded in October 1975, all three returned to the NFL. Neither Kiick nor Warfield rejoined the Dolphins but Csonka eventually returned for his final season in 1979. Csonka actually had a chance to return to the Dolphins for the tail end of the 1975 season but his agent and Dolphins owner Joe Robbie did not have a great relationship and negotiations broke down before the roster freeze deadline.

4. Csonka and Mercury Morris made some more history during the perfect season of 1972. The duo became the first teammates to ever rush for 1,000 yards in a season, leading Miami to break the NFL's rushing record in the process. It was the second of three straight 1,000-yard seasons for Csonka, but the 1,000 yards that Morris ran for in 1972 was the only time he reached the threshold.

5. For 24 years, Delvin Williams held the Dolphins record for most rushing yards in a season as the first Miami running back to rush for 1,200 yards. It was quite the first impression for Williams in Miami after the Dolphins traded a lot to acquire him from San Francisco. The next two years were a struggle, however, as he ran for just 1,374 yards and five touchdowns in 29 games played.

6. Karim Abdul-Jabbar set almost all of the Dolphins rookie rushing records after being a third-round pick in the 1996 draft. He is the only Miami rookie running back to run for 1,000 yards in a season, his 11 touchdowns as a rookie tied

the franchise record, and he had the most 100-yard rushing games by a rookie with four. His name, though, caused him the biggest problem despite the fact he had no control over it. The name was chosen for him by his imam, the Islamic prayer leader, and he knew it would raise some eyebrows when he entered the league. What he might not have expected was to be sued by Basketball Hall-of-Famer Kareem Abdul-Jabbar and being forced to legally change his name to Abdul-Karim al-Jabbar as a result of the lawsuit.

7. Ricky Williams left the Dolphins in a lurch when he unexpectedly retired two days before training camp in 2004. Williams was coming off consecutive seasons with at least 1,300 rushing yards that still rank first and second in team history and seemed to be getting his NFL career on track after struggling in New Orleans. However, reporters discovered that Williams failed a third drug test for marijuana and the impending four-game suspension might have been a reason for Williams to retire. However, he returned to the team in 2005 after a year off, served that suspension, and then was suspended for all of 2006 for another drug violation. He had one more 1,000-yard season in 2009 before retiring from the NFL in 2011 after spending the year in Baltimore.

8. Ronnie Brown's historic day on September 21, 2008, was made even more special by the fact the Dolphins weren't running a normal offense. Yes, Miami had Chad Pennington playing quarterback most of the time but that

41

day Brown ran for r touchdowns while also playing quarterback for many plays. That game was the modern debut of the Wildcat offense, in which Brown would line up at quarterback and run the same basic six plays with Williams as his accomplice in the backfield. Brown ran 17 times for 113 yards against the Patriots and even threw a 19-yard touchdown pass to Anthony Fasano out of the Wildcat formation.

9. The Dolphins have excelled at finding quality starting running backs in the later rounds of the draft. Kiick was a fifth-round pick in 1968, the same year Miami selected Csonka in the first round. Miami drafted Lamar Miller in the fourth round in 2012 and Miller ran for nearly 1,100 yards in 2014 before leaving the Dolphins in free agency. In 2015, the Dolphins scooped up Jay Ajayi in the fifth round and rode him to nearly 1,300 yards in 2012 before trading him in the middle of the following season. The starter entering 2020 was Myles Gaskin, a seventh-round pick in 2019.

10. It was a rough year for the Dolphins rushing attack in 2019 as Ryan Fitzpatrick became the first quarterback to lead the team in rushing. His 243 rushing yards was the lowest ever to lead the team, dipping below the 274 yards Abner Haynes had in 1967 to lead Miami in rushing. As a team, Miami ran for just 1,156 yards, by far the lowest the Dolphins have had in a season and a total that would rank fifth on the Dolphins' single-season rushing list for an individual.

CHAPTER 5:

CATCHING THE BALL

QUIZ TIME!

1. Which of the following receivers never led the NFL in receiving touchdowns?

    a. Paul Warfield
    b. Mark Clayton
    c. Nat Moore
    d. McDuffie

2. Who holds the Miami record for most career 100-yard receiving games?

    a. Mark Clayton
    b. Mark Duper
    c. Paul Warfield
    d. Chris Chambers

3. In 2012, which receiver set the Dolphins record with 253 receiving yards against the Arizona Cardinals?

    a. Davone Bess
    b. Mike Wallace

  c. Brian Hartline

  d. Brandon Marshall

4. Which player did not catch a pass from both Bob Griese and Dan Marino?

  a. Nat Moore

  b. Tony Nathan

  c. Bruce Hardy

  d. Terry Robiskie

5. Ted Ginn Jr. holds the Dolphins record for most receiving yards in a game without a touchdown with 175 yards.

  a. True

  b. False

6. Who was the last non-wide receiver to lead the Dolphins in receptions in a season?

  a. Randy McMichael

  b. Terry Kirby

  c. Charles Clay

  d. Jim Kiick

7. Who is the only receiver in Dolphins history to go over 100 receiving yards in four straight games?

  a. Brian Hartline

  b. Mark Clayton

  c. Oronde Gadsden

  d. Irving Fryar

8. Which receiver holds the Dolphins record for most receptions in a single game with 15?

a. Jarvis Landry

b. Mark Clayton

c. Chris Chambers

d. McDuffie

9. Mark Ingram and Paul Warfield share the Dolphins record of 4 touchdown catches in a game.

a. True

b. False

10. Which of these receivers did the Dolphins not draft?

a. Mark Duper

b. Jarvis Landry

c. Brian Hartline

d. Wes Welker

11. In which season was Paul Warfield not an All-Pro receiver for the Dolphins?

a. 1971

b. 1972

c. 1973

d. 1974

12. What was the most receiving yards Paul Warfield ever had with the Dolphins?

a. 983 yards

b. 992 yards

c. 996 yards

d. 999 yards

13. How many consecutive seasons did Nat Moore lead the Dolphins in receptions?

    a. 4
    b. 5
    c. 6
    d. 7

14. Who was the Dolphins' first 1,000-yard receiver?

    a. Duriel Harris
    b. Nat Moore
    c. Mark Clayton
    d. Mark Duper

15. Mark Clayton and Mark Duper both had more than 1,300 receiving yards in 1984 and those marks seasons still rank first and second in Dolphins history.

    a. True
    b. False

16. How long is Mark Clayton's franchise record for most consecutive games with a catch?

    a. 92 games
    b. 94 games
    c. 95 games
    d. 97 games

17. In which year did O.J. McDuffie have the only 1,000-yard season in his career?

    a. 1996
    b. 1997

c. 1998

d. 1999

18. What injury ended O.J. McDuffie's career prematurely after the 2000 season?

   a. Toe

   b. Knee

   c. Shoulder

   d. Head

19. Jarvis Landry holds the top-three spots on Miami's single-season receptions list.

   a. True

   b. False

20. How many times, including playoffs, did Jarvis Landry catch 10 or more passes in a game for the Dolphins?

   a. 7

   b. 8

   c. 9

   d. 10

QUIZ ANSWERS

1. D – O.J. McDuffie

2. B – Mark Duper

3. C – Brian Hartline

4. D – Terry Robiskie

5. A – True

6. A – Randy McMichael

7. D – Irving Fryar

8. C – Chris Chambers

9. A – True

10. D – Wes Welker

11. D – 1974

12. C – 996 yards

13. C – 6

14. D – Mark Duper

15. B – False

16. A – 92 games

17. C – 1998

18. A – Toe

19. A – True

20. B – 8

DID YOU KNOW?

1. Paul Warfield might have sealed his Hall of Fame credentials in his four seasons with the Dolphins, but the Ohio native was not pleased to be traded to Miami from his hometown Cleveland Browns. When he reflected 30 years after the trade, he said that the deal was a "jolt" and "I have to admit going to Miami was not a place I desired to go." But when he returned to Cleveland in 1973 as a member of the Dolphins, he received a standing ovation and loud roars of approval from the crowd when he was introduced. Don Shula even mentioned to him on the sideline how touched he was by the gesture, and Warfield called that moment one of the highlights of his career.

2. Nat Moore holds the Dolphins record of leading Miami in receptions for six straight seasons, taking over the mantle once Warfield defected to the World Football League in 1975. But he is perhaps most known in Dolphins lore for his "Helicopter Catch" in 1984 against the Jets. Moore had fumbled earlier in the game when he went over the middle on the exact same play deep in Jets territory. He caught the ball inside the 10-yard line and turned upfield trying to score a touchdown when he was hit by Ken Schroy and Kirk Springs, flipping him in the air short of the goal line. He told the team website in 2019, "The only thing that was going through my mind was whatever I do, do not let the damn ball go because then I'll have to see Shula again. I

was only thinking to hold on to the football. There's no way in the world I was going to have to go see Shula because I fumbled again. When I'm spinning, I'm thinking just to not let it go."

3. The 1980s for the Miami Dolphins were defined mostly by Dan Marino and his two leading receivers, the Marks Brothers. Mark Duper and Mark Clayton still rank first and second in career receiving yards and receptions for the Dolphins and were the main weapons for Marino early in his career. When the Dolphins released Duper in 1993, he and Clayton had each gone over 1,000 yards receiving in three different seasons (1984, 1986, and 1991), tying the NFL record for most multiple 1,000-yard seasons by teammates.

4. When the Marks Brothers were honored in 2003 by being inducted into the Dolphins Honor Roll, Marino shared a story about how Clayton won Miami a game in 1991 against the Bears. According to Marino, the biting wind was making the players miserable so Clayton told Marino to throw the ball deep and he would end the game right there. Clayton warned that he would run to the locker room right after winning the game, however. Marino listened to his receiver and him on a deep pass that Clayton slid to catch at the five-yard line. He calmly planted the ball at the spot where Miami would eventually kick the game-winning field goal then ran to the locker room to get warm.

5. Oronde Gadsden came to the Dolphins in 1998 as a 27-year-old rookie who had bounced around many places after graduating from Winston-Salem State. He was signed as an undrafted free agent by the Cowboys in 1995 and was a member of the team's practice squad when they won the Super Bowl that season. He was promoted to the active roster for the NFC Championship game that season but sprained his ankle and missed the Super Bowl. He broke a bone near his right eye before training camp in 1996 and then signed with the Steelers for training camp. He had a tryout to play in NFL Europe in 1997 but separated his shoulder during the tryout. So, he instead played in the Arena Football League and was named the Rookie of the Year after catching 37 touchdown passes. To top it off, his first career NFL catch was a 44-yard touchdown, landing him a starting spot the following week.

6. O.J. McDuffie's career unfortunately ended in 2001 due to a toe injury, which became the issue in a legal battle between McDuffie and the Dolphins team doctor. McDuffie played in just nine games in 2000 due to the injury and didn't dress at all in 2001 before Miami cut him. In 2010, McDuffie won an $11.5 million verdict against Dr. John Uribe for negligence and medical malpractice for the way Uribe treated McDuffie's toe injury in 1999. However, that verdict was thrown out on appeal and McDuffie lost the retrial in 2018 as well as the appeal in 2020.

7. The lawsuit has not soured McDuffie's love for the franchise, however. He has hosted a podcast about the

Dolphins since 2018 with Seth Levit called "The Fish Tank" in which Levit and McDuffie interview various former players, media members, and team executives about the Dolphins. Former guests include Larry Csonka, Mercury Morris, Patrick Surtain, and Zach Thomas as they dish about the best Dolphins stories you've never heard before.

8. The day Chris Chambers set the Dolphins record for most receptions in the game was memorable in many ways. The star receiver was targeted 26 times in that December 4, 2005, game against the Bills in Miami and hauled in 15 of those passes. But it was his 15th and final catch that will stick out in the minds of Dolphins fans because the 4-yard touchdown grab with six seconds left helped Miami complete a 21-point fourth-quarter comeback to stun Buffalo 24-23. The 238 yards Chambers had that game also stood as the Dolphins' single-game record for seven years before it was broken by Brian Hartline.

9. Brandon Marshall's two seasons in Miami were literally life-changing for the wide receiver. After leading the Dolphins in receiving in 2010, Marshall was confronted by his agent and personal assistant about his mental health issues. The intervention led to a diagnosis of borderline personality disorder, which he shared publicly in training camp before the 2011 season. He said he had sought counseling and therapy for most of his first four seasons in the NFL, but that it did little to help him. It was only a three-month stay at McLean Hospital in Boston that

helped him understand his struggles and the root cause of it all. In his post-football life, Marshall is a strong mental health advocate and runs a mental health non-profit called Project 375.

10. Jarvis Landry's talent was never an issue with the Dolphins, but his temperament on the field got him shipped out of town. He had consecutive 1,100-yard seasons for the Dolphins in 2015 and 2016, but the team was frustrated with Landry's inability to control his emotions on the field. It all came to a head in the 2017 season finale when Landry was ejected for fighting Bills safety Jordan Poyer in the fourth quarter. That was his final game with Miami; the Dolphins traded Landry to Cleveland in the offseason.

CHAPTER 6:

TRENCH WARFARE

QUIZ TIME!

1. Which offensive lineman did not play 10 or more years for the Dolphins?

    a. Ed Newman

    b. Bob Kuechenberg

    c. Dwight Stephenson

    d. Richmond Webb

2. Who did not make 150 or more career starts for the Dolphins?

    a. Bob Kuechenberg

    b. Richmond Webb

    c. Tim Ruddy

    d. Larry Little

3. Which offensive lineman did not make five or more Pro Bowls during his Dolphins career?

    a. Jim Langer

    b. Ed Newman

c. Dwight Stephenson

d. Richmond Webb

4. Which of these offensive linemen did Miami draft?

   a. Larry Little

   b. Bob Kuechenberg

   c. Jim Langer

   d. Richmond Webb

5. Who else started at left tackle for Miami during its perfect 1972 season aside from Super Bowl VII starter Wayne Moore?

   a. Doug Crusan

   b. Norm Evans

   c. Al Jenkins

   d. Bob Kuechenberg

6. Who was the only offensive lineman who was on the roster for Miami's first game and its first Super Bowl championship?

   a. Doug Crusan

   b. Maxie Williams

   c. Billy Neighbors

   d. Norm Evans

7. Who was not a first-team selection for an NFL All-Decade team?

   a. Richmond Webb

   b. Dwight Stephenson

   c. Jim Langer

   d. Larry Little

8. Jake Long is the only offensive lineman the Dolphins have picked in the top 10 of the NFL draft.

   a. True
   b. False

9. How many Super Bowls did Bob Kuechenberg start during his Dolphins career?

   a. 2
   b. 3
   c. 4
   d. 5

10. Both Super Bowl championship teams featured the same starting five offensive linemen in the Super Bowl.

   a. True
   b. False

11. What is the Dolphins' record for most sacks in a single season?

   a. 18.5
   b. 19
   c. 19.5
   d. 20

12. Who is the only player in Dolphins history to have 5 sacks in a game twice?

   a. Vern Den Herder
   b. Jason Taylor
   c. Cameron Wake
   d. Bill Stanfill

13. Who was Miami playing in 1973 when it set the franchise record with 9 sacks in a game?

    a. Kansas City Chiefs

    b. Buffalo Bills

    c. Baltimore Colts

    d. New England Patriots

14. In which year did Doug Betters become the first Dolphins defensive lineman to be named the Associated Press' Defensive Player of the Year?

    a. 1982

    b. 1983

    c. 1984

    d. 1985

15. Nick Buoniconti was never a first-team All-Pro during his career with the Dolphins.

    a. True

    b. False

16. How many times was Zach Thomas named a first-team All-Pro linebacker by the Associated Press?

    a. 3

    b. 4

    c. 5

    d. 6

17. How many fumbles did Jason Taylor recover during his career in Miami?

    a. 23

    b. 24

c. 27

d. 29

18. How many sacks did Jason Taylor have as a Dolphin?

    a. 128

    b. 131

    c. 135

    d. 139

19. Jason Taylor holds the records for the longest and shortest defensive touchdowns in Dolphins history.

    a. True

    b. False

20. Who is the only Dolphins player to ever score a defensive 2-point conversion?

    a. Lloyd Mumphord

    b. Curtis Johnson

    c. Jordan Phillips

    d. Walt Aikens

QUIZ ANSWERS

1. C – Dwight Stephenson

2. C – Tim Ruddy

3. B – Ed Newman

4. D – Richmond Webb

5. A – Doug Crusan

6. D – Norm Evans

7. A – Richmond Webb

8. B – False

9. C – 4

10. A – True

11. A – 18.5

12. D – Bill Stanfill

13. B – Buffalo Bills

14. B – 1983

15. A – True

16. C – 5

17. C – 27

18. B – 131

19. B – False

20. D – Walt Aikens

DID YOU KNOW?

1. Bob Kuechenberg played in Super Bowl VIII with a broken arm held together by a metal rod. Kuechenberg had broken the arm late in the season and was upset when the team doctor, Charles Virgin, pulled him from the game. The guard told the doctor to find a plan so he could play in the playoffs, so Virgin put the metal rod in Kuechenberg's arm and fitted him for a cast. Kuechenberg played an all-time great game in neutralizing Minnesota's Alan Page, the Defensive Player of the Year that season, as the Dolphins won their second straight Super Bowl.

2. All it took for Larry Little's career to take off in Miami was a note from Don Shula. Little's first interaction with the legendary coach after he was named to lead the Dolphins was short but memorable. Little introduced himself to Shula, who quickly asked him how much he weighed. When Little replied 285 pounds, Shula just shook his head and walked away. A few weeks later, Little received a letter telling him to report to training camp at 265 pounds or he'd face a $10 per pound per day penalty. He shed the 20 pounds and went on to be named to five consecutive All-Pro teams from 1971 through 1975.

3. Jim Langer's Hall of Fame career was nearly derailed before it even began in Miami. He joined the Dolphins as a free agent in 1970 and, leading up to the perfect 1972

season, Dolphins offensive line coach Monte Clark would tell Shula that Langer should be the starting center, but Shula ignored him. The head coach preferred three-time Pro Bowler Bob DeMarco but, after Langer shone in the preseason, he took every snap in the 1972 season and went on to appear in 128 straight games for the Dolphins.

4. Richmond Webb made a name for himself as the starting left tackle protecting Dan Marino's blind side for most of the 1990s. But it was a different Webb stepping into the spotlight in 2019 when Richmond's cousin, J'Marcus, took over at tackle for the Dolphins. The Miami coaches even call J'Marcus "Richmond," as a joke, but there is a lot of pressure given what Richmond Webb did in Miami. He was *The Sporting News'* Rookie of the Year in 1990 and broke the record for most consecutive starts in 1997. He is also one of five offensive linemen on the Dolphins Honor Roll.

5. All of these years later, Bill Stanfill's name still fills the Dolphins' record books. If there is a single-season or single-game sack record to be had, chances are it belongs to Stanfill, Miami's first pass rushing wizard. He set the record for most sacks in a game in 1972 and then tied himself for the record the following year. His single-season record for sacks has stood since 1973, though it was tied by Jason Taylor almost 30 years later. He also holds the mark for most sacks in a season by a rookie, with 8 in his debut season in 1969.

6. Before his trade from the Patriots to the Dolphins in 1969, Nick Buoniconti was getting ready to retire from the NFL. He was growing tired of football and he had worked hard to obtain his law degree while playing for New England. He had even signed a lease to open up a law firm in the Boston area. After the trade to Miami, Buoniconti acted as his own agent and demanded Joe Robbie double his pay and make the salary guaranteed. When Robbie refused, Buoniconti filed retirement papers and committed himself to the law firm. Robbie eventually cracked under the pressure and Buoniconti became the leader of Miami's defense that won consecutive Super Bowl titles in the 1970s.

7. Bob Baumhower was drafted by Miami as a defensive end but, early in offseason workouts, Don Shula wanted to switch him to nose guard. It was a change that Baumhower did not like and it became evident to the coaches during training camp. After the first week, Shula had a conversation with Baumhower, telling him that he could be a good defensive end in the NFL but he thought Baumhower could be a great nose tackle. After that conversation, Baumhower said he committed himself to mastering the position, and the hard work paid off as Baumhower ended up being a five-time Pro Bowler and 1983 first-team All-Pro at the position while anchoring the Dolphins' Killer Bs Defense.

8. Zach Thomas' nickname when he first arrived in Miami was the "Baby Elephant." The reason for the funky

nickname was that Thomas tried to soak up as much knowledge and advice as possible from Trace Armstrong, so he followed him around the facility. Thomas even went as far as to hire the same stretch therapist and financial advisor as Armstrong. Whatever he picked up from Armstrong worked, because Thomas was a finalist for the Pro Football Hall of Fame in 2020.

9. Jason Taylor's Hall of Fame career almost ended three years earlier and with one fewer leg. During his one season in Washington in 2008, Taylor was leg whipped, a common occurrence when you're playing on the defensive line in the NFL. The area was sore and some postgame pain medicine helped numb the pain but, when the medication wore off, Taylor struggled to fall asleep. Taylor called the trainer to see if he could take another pain pill but was told he shouldn't. The trainer ended up rushing to Taylor's house and immediately took him to the hospital where his blood pressure tested off the charts. The doctors wanted to do immediate surgery but Taylor said he wanted a second opinion. When he called the famous Dr. James Andrews, Andrews also suggested surgery and said if Taylor waited to fly to Andrews in the morning, Andrews would have to amputate the leg. The issue was compartment syndrome, in which the muscle bleeds into the body cavity and causes nerve damage, so Taylor was a few hours away from amputation.

10. Cameron Wake went undrafted out of Penn State and then didn't make it out of training camp with the Giants as a

free agent. So he went to Canada and dominated the Canadian Football League for two seasons. He led the CFL in sacks in 2007 and 2008 and was a two-time Defensive Player of the Year. Wake totaled 16 sacks as a rookie to become the first player to be named the CFL's Rookie of the Year and Defensive Player of the Year and he followed up that performance with 23 sacks in 2008. It was then that the Dolphins took notice and signed Wake, who racked up 98 sacks with Miami.

CHAPTER 7:

NO AIR ZONE

QUIZ TIME!

1. Who set the Dolphins record with 10 interceptions in a single season?

    a. Troy Vincent
    b. Jake Scott
    c. Dick Westmoreland
    d. Dick Anderson

2. Which linebacker is tied with Reshad Jones for most interceptions returned for touchdowns in franchise history?

    a. Zach Thomas
    b. Nick Buoniconti
    c. Cameron Wake
    d. A.J. Duhe

3. Who holds Miami's single-game record with 4 interceptions?

    a. Dick Anderson
    b. Sam Madison

c. Tim Foley

d. Patrick Surtain

4. Brock Marion holds the Dolphin record for the longest interception returned for a touchdown with a 100-yard return against Buffalo in 2002

   a. True

   b. False

5. Which of these players did not intercept 30 passes during his Dolphins career?

   a. Dick Anderson

   b. Jake Scott

   c. Patrick Surtain

   d. Sam Madison

6. How many times has a Dolphins player led or tied for the league lead in interceptions in a season?

   a. 1

   b. 2

   c. 3

   d. 4

7. The Dolphins have led the NFL in fewest passing yards allowed three times. Which was not one of the years in which Miami led the league?

   a. 1972

   b. 1982

   c. 1991

   d. 2001

8. The Dolphins have never had two first-team Associated Press All-Pro secondary players in the same season.

    a. True
    b. False

9. How many first- or second-team Associated Press All-Pro defensive backs has Miami had in its history?

    a. 3
    b. 4
    c. 5
    d. 6

10. Who is the only Dolphins defensive back to earn a spot on an NFL All-Decade team?

    a. Jake Scott
    b. Troy Vincent
    c. Glenn Blackwood
    d. Dick Anderson

11. The Dolphins named seven defensive backs to their 50th-anniversary team.

    a. True
    b. False

12. In which season was Dick Anderson named the NFL Defensive Player of the Year?

    a. 1972
    b. 1973
    c. 1974
    d. 1975

13. Dick Anderson made an immediate impact on the Dolphins with how many interceptions as a rookie in 1968?

    a. 5

    b. 6

    c. 7

    d. 8

14. Dick Westmoreland set the team record with interceptions in how many consecutive games?

    a. 3

    b. 4

    c. 5

    d. 6

15. Which defensive back did not have 10 takeaways in a season for Miami?

    a. Dick Anderson

    b. Glenn Blackwood

    c. Jake Scott

    d. Dick Westmoreland

16. In which year did the Dolphins set the team record with 32 interceptions in a season?

    a. 1970

    b. 1978

    c. 1985

    d. 1999

17. Miami has intercepted 6 passes in a game six times but against five different opponents. Against which have the Dolphins done it twice?

    a. Baltimore Colts
    b. Buffalo Bills
    c. New York Jets
    d. Pittsburgh Steelers

18. Which quarterback have the Dolphins intercepted the most in their history?

    a. Joe Namath
    b. Tom Brady
    c. Drew Bledsoe
    d. Joe Ferguson

19. For five seasons from 2000-2004, Sam Madison and Patrick Surtain started 73 out of a possible 80 regular-season games together. Which cornerback started four of those seven games the tandem was not intact?

    a. Terrell Buckley
    b. Will Poole
    c. Terry Cousin
    d. Jamar Fletcher

20. Sam Madison won a Super Bowl as a player after leaving the Dolphins.

    a. True
    b. False

QUIZ ANSWERS

1. C – Dick Westmoreland

2. A – Zach Thomas

3. A – Dick Anderson

4. B – False

5. C – Patrick Surtain

6. D – 4

7. C – 1991

8. B – False

9. D – 6

10. D – Dick Anderson

11. A – True

12. B – 1973

13. D – 8

14. C – 5

15. B – Glenn Blackwood

16. B – 1978

17. C – New York Jets

18. D – Joe Ferguson

19. D – Jamar Fletcher

20. A – True

DID YOU KNOW?

1. Jake Scott's tenure in Miami ended on a sour note because of his dislike of new defensive coordinator Vince Costello. Bill Arnsparger was well-liked and respected by the Dolphins defenders during his tenure as the team's defensive coordinator but, when he became the Giants head coach, Costello took over the defense. His plays were often overruled and changed on the field by veteran members of Miami's defense but the play-calling stuck with Scott. One day in 1976, the anger in Scott boiled over and he cussed out Costello. Don Shula tried to intervene, and Scott cussed at him, too. Five days later, Shula traded Scott to Washington.

2. Dick Anderson's greatest individual moment came late in the 1973 season when the Pittsburgh Steelers visited the Orange Bowl. In the first half of that Monday Night Football game in December, Anderson intercepted four passes and returned two of them for touchdowns as the Dolphins stormed out to a 30-3 lead at halftime. Anderson took the first interception back 27 yards for a score just 1:04 into the game and then added a 38-yard touchdown return early in the second quarter to put Miami up 27-0 a little more than 16 minutes into the game. The performance is still tied for the NFL record for interceptions in a game and interceptions returned for touchdowns in a game. The

Dolphins held on to win the game in the second half en route to their second consecutive Super Bowl title.

3. Dick Westmoreland intercepted 10 passes in 1967, Miami's second season of existence, and no one has hit the double-digit mark since then. Five different players, including Anderson three times, have had eight interceptions in a season, but no one has touched Westmoreland's record. He had four picks in the Dolphins' inaugural season and he had one more in 1968 to finish his Dolphins career with 15 career interceptions.

4. Tim Foley made the conscious choice to remove himself from public life in connection with his football career after his retirement. He was a color commentator on TBS' college football broadcasts for 15 years, but he rarely made other appearances as it related to his career in the NFL. He also owned a multi-million-dollar marketing business through Amway but has kept a low-profile otherwise and stayed out of the spotlight whenever possible.

5. Glenn Blackwood patrolled the Dolphins secondary for nine seasons as one of the team's starting safeties, and Miami has the World Football League to thank for that. When the WFL folded in 1975, the NFL rights to the three Dolphins players who defected were still owned by Miami. When they all signed with different teams, Miami received draft compensation in return. The eighth-round selection the Dolphins received from Denver when it signed Jim Kiick was used to draft Blackwood, who finished with 29 interceptions in Miami.

6. Lloyd Mumphord is one of just two players the Dolphins drafted in the 16th round or later to play for Miami. The 16th-round selection in 1969 out of Texas Southern finished his Dolphins career with 14 interceptions, including five as a rookie in 1969 and five more in his second year in 1970 before being supplanted as a starter by Foley.

7. Patrick Surtain is known now in Florida for his successful stint as the head coach at local powerhouse American Heritage School. Surtain's teams are known for running former Dolphins coach Jimmy Johnson's physical style of defense with pressing cornerbacks, similar to what Surtain was in Miami. Surtain began as an assistant with the school and took over as head coach in 2016, leading the Patriots to back-to-back state titles in his first two seasons.

8. A part of Sam Madison will always live with his teenage daughter, Kennedy. In 2015, Kennedy started to go into kidney failure at the age of 11 and was put on a transplant list. However, she was taken off the list after suffering a blood clot near her heart that made the transplant impossible. By the time she recovered, she was so far down the list that someone suggested Madison donate his kidney to his daughter. He was a perfect match and, in September 2016, Sam donated a kidney to his daughter. He interviewed for a job with the Dolphins in 2019, but when he was passed over for the position, the Chiefs called and he was able to win a Super Bowl ring with Kansas City in Miami that season.

9. Troy Vincent had a pretty memorable first day in Miami after being selected with the seventh overall pick in the 1992 NFL draft. Don Shula picked up Vincent in his Crowne Victoria and drove him to the facility for the first time. In the car ride, Shula told Vincent to seek out number 56, John Offerdahl, to let him teach Vincent how to be a professional football player. Later in that same car ride, Shula told Vincent that he could hide him for two years before teams would expose his weaknesses, so he needed to be a student of the game. The message was confusing at first but, with Offerdahl's guidance and some experience in the league, Vincent said the lesson made a lot more sense as he matured.

10. Curtis Johnson is the Dolphins' all-time leader in blocked kicks with 9. He blocked 6 field goals, 1 extra point, and 2 punts. The only person with more blocked field goals than Johnson is Mumphord, who blocked 7 field goals in his six seasons in Miami.

CHAPTER 8:

SUPER BOWL SALUTE

QUIZ TIME!

1. Which is the only team Miami has faced twice in the Super Bowl?

    a. Washington Redskins
    b. Dallas Cowboys
    c. San Francisco 49ers
    d. Minnesota Vikings

2. How would you express the result in Roman numerals if you added all of the Super Bowl numbers Miami has appeared in?

    a. XLIII
    b. XLV
    c. XLVII
    d. XLIX

3. How many times has the Dolphins' home stadium hosted the Super Bowl?

    a. 9
    b. 10

c. 11

d. 12

4. How many different stadiums hosted the Miami Dolphins' Super Bowl appearances?

    a. 2

    b. 3

    c. 4

    d. 5

5. One of the Dolphins' Super Bowls was played in February.

    a. True

    b. False

6. What is the most points the Dolphins allowed in one of their five Super Bowl appearances?

    a. 27

    b. 28

    c. 34

    d. 38

7. Which Dolphins offensive lineman started four of Miami's five Super Bowls?

    a. Bob Kuechenberg

    b. Larry Little

    c. Norm Evans

    d. Jim Langer

8. Miami held the record for fewest points scored by a Super Bowl winner for 46 years until it was broken by the Patriots.

a. True

b. False

9. How many turnovers did Miami have in its Super Bowl VI loss to the Cowboys?

    a. 1

    b. 2

    c. 3

    d. 4

10. How long was Garo Yepremian's field goal at the end of the first half of Super Bowl VI for Miami's first points in a Super Bowl?

    a. 28 yards

    b. 31 yards

    c. 36 yards

    d. 42 yards

11. Who scored the first touchdown in a Super Bowl in Dolphins history?

    a. Bob Griese

    b. Howard Twilley

    c. Jim Kiick

    d. Mercury Morris

12. Who was not credited with a takeaway in Super Bowl VII against Washington?

    a. Jake Scott

    b. Dick Anderson

    c. Nick Buoniconti

    d. Manny Fernandez

13. Jake Scott was the first defensive player to be named Super Bowl MVP.

    a. True
    b. False

14. How many times did Bob Griese throw the ball in Miami's two Super Bowl victories?

    a. 18
    b. 22
    c. 25
    d. 29

15. What was the longest run Larry Csonka had in Super Bowl VIII against the Vikings?

    a. 10 yards
    b. 13 yards
    c. 16 yards
    d. 19 yards

16. Who had an interception for the only turnover Miami forced off Minnesota in Super Bowl VIII?

    a. Bill Stanfill
    b. Lloyd Mumphord
    c. Jake Scott
    d. Curtis Johnson

17. How many first downs did Miami gain in its Super Bowl XVII loss to Washington?

    a. 15
    b. 13

c. 11

d. 9

18. Super Bowl XVII was the only Super Bowl that Miami lost in which it held a lead.

   a. True

   b. False

19. Who caught the only touchdown Miami scored in its loss to San Francisco in Super Bowl XIX?

   a. Mark Clayton

   b. Tony Nathan

   c. Dan Johnson

   d. Nat Moore

20. Joe Montana was the only quarterback to throw for more than 200 yards against the Dolphins in the Super Bowl with 331 passing yards in Super Bowl XIX. Who threw the next most passing yards on Miami in a Super Bowl?

   a. Roger Staubach

   b. Fran Tarkenton

   c. Joe Theismann

   d. Billy Kilmer

QUIZ ANSWERS

1. A – Washington Redskins

2. C – XLVII

3. C – 11

4. D – 5

5. B – False

6. D – 38

7. A – Bob Kuechenberg

8. A – True

9. C – 3

10. B – 31 yards

11. B – Howard Twilley

12. D – Manny Fernandez

13. B – False

14. A – 18

15. C – 16 yards

16. D – Curtis Johnson

17. D – 9

18. B – False

19. C – Dan Johnson

20. B – Fran Tarkenton

DID YOU KNOW?

1. The path to Miami's first Super Bowl appearance in 1971 was marked by history. The Dolphins defeated Kansas City in the longest game in NFL history, a divisional round playoff game that lasted more than 82 minutes before Garo Yepremian kicked the winning field goal. The Chiefs led 10-0 after the first quarter, but the Dolphins responded to tie the game at halftime. Kansas City held a one-TD lead late in the fourth quarter, but Miami scored with 1:25 left to tie the game. A long Chiefs return set up a chance at a winning field goal, but Kansas City missed it. Both teams missed field goals in the first overtime period as well before Yepremian knocked home the 37-yarder to win.

2. The success of the 1972 Miami Dolphins began in Super Bowl VI the previous year. Miami's loss to Dallas was so disheartening for the young Dolphins that it became a motivation for the 1972 team. Even after defeating Washington to win Super Bowl VII, many Dolphins were thinking about losing the previous year. "The thing I thought about was redemption," Manny Fernandez told the *Miami Herald*. Dick Anderson used the word "relief" to describe that Super Bowl VII victory. And it all began the first day back from that loss when Shula showed the Dolphins film from that loss to Dallas and told them "You see how sick and sorry you feel now? Well, just think how

sick and sorry you'll continue to feel if you don't go back and redeem yourselves for what you did last year."

3. One of the most famous gaffes in Super Bowl history occurred in Super Bowl VII with Yepremian's unfortunate throw that led to Washington's only score. The Dolphins kicker felt bad about ruining the 1972 team's chance to have the first – and only – shutout in Super Bowl history despite Miami's win over Washington. However, he was able to forgive himself after receiving a letter from coach Don Shula. The problem? Shula did not recall ever sending that letter. It was actually Shula's wife, Dorothy, who sent the letter to the kicker to help him feel better about the mistake.

4. Larry Csonka got the sense that Shula was becoming increasingly tense during the Dolphins' perfect season in 1972, so he devised a prank to help loosen up the coach. He and Manny Fernandez wrangled a three-foot gator into Shula's private shower after practice and, when Shula discovered it, he ran away and ordered an assistant to catch the reptile. An equipment manager dealt with the issue and an irate Shula angrily asked who was behind the prank. Before anyone could speak up, Shula burst into laughter over the incident.

5. Many people will remember the parting shot of Shula being carried off the field after winning Super Bowl VII. But if you watch the video closely, you'll see someone stole Shula's watch in the celebration. Years later, Shula said that he could feel someone grabbing his hand, but he

couldn't see who it was. It wasn't until he returned to the locker room that he realized that someone had stolen his Rolex.

6. Many people would argue that the Dolphins' 1973 team was better than the one that went unbeaten the year before. Miami played a much more difficult schedule in 1973 than in 1972 and, though that team lost two games, the Dolphins felt they were more dominant in 1973 than in 1972. The players said it had to do with their maturation and experience after the previous seasons, along with the fact that Miami received every team's best shot after going undefeated and winning the Super Bowl. As Paul Warfield put it, "A lot of the guys on the teams were the same but we were a more polished team and more mature team. We had understood the concept of winning when everybody was gunning to try to beat us. We were a better team in 1973."

7. Miami quarterback David Woodley had arguably the worst performance in Super Bowl history in Super Bowl XVII for the Dolphins. He completed just 4 of 14 passes and threw for just 97 yards, 76 of which came on one touchdown throw to Jimmy Cefalo in the first quarter. He was unable to rally Miami in the second half of the game as Washington came back and pulled away for an easy victory.

8. No one doubts Shula's credentials as a coach but his teams struggled to win championships. With the loss to San Francisco in Super Bowl XIX, Shula tied Bud Grant with

four losses in the big game. Three of those defeats came with the Dolphins in a 14-year period in which he led Miami to their five Super Bowl appearances.

9. The 1972 Dolphins never had the chance to meet the president after completing their perfect season, as has become customary for sports championship teams. But, in 2013, 31 members of the 1972 team met with Barack Obama thanks to a connection with Marv Fleming. The meeting included a funny moment when Obama was talking about his visit a few years earlier with the 1985 Bears and Shula interrupted the president to remind him that Miami was the only team to beat Chicago that season. Shula just had to settle for phone calls from President Richard Nixon, who spent time in Key Biscayne during his presidency and was a noted sports fan.

10. The Dolphins have played in five Super Bowls and Miami's performances have steadily declined in each quarter. Miami has outscored its foes 38-10 in the first quarter, but the Dolphins have lost the second quarter 38-29, lost the third 20-7, and they were blanked 35-0 in the fourth quarter of those games.

CHAPTER 9:

SHINING THE BUSTS

QUIZ TIME!

1. What was the only year in which the Dolphins had two players inducted into the Hall of Fame?

   a. 1983

   b. 1987

   c. 1990

   d. 1993

2. How many times did Paul Warfield have 30 catches in a season for the Dolphins?

   a. 1

   b. 2

   c. 3

   d. 4

3. What position did Jim Langer play at South Dakota State before finding his place at center for the Dolphins?

   a. Offensive tackle

   b. Defensive end

c. Linebacker

d. Tight end

4. Nick Buoniconti and Jim Langer were the first two former Dolphins players to be honored with a helmet sticker after their deaths in 2019.

   a. True

   b. False

5. Larry Csonka set a career high in 1979, his final year with the Dolphins, when he ran for how many touchdowns?

   a. 9

   b. 10

   c. 11

   d. 12

6. Larry Csonka was known for his sure hands while carrying the football. How many fumbles did he finish his career with over 11 seasons?

   a. 17

   b. 19

   c. 21

   d. 23

7. What was Bob Griese's best single-season completion percentage with the Dolphins?

   a. 61.8 percent

   b. 63 percent

   c. 64.9 percent

   d. 65.5 percent

8. Griese's career-ending shoulder injury came in the same game in which he passed 25,000 career passing yards.

    a. True

    b. False

9. How much was the signing bonus the Chargers paid Larry Little when they signed him out of Bethune Cookman?

    a. $0

    b. $500

    c. $750

    d. $1,000

10. Perhaps grossly underappreciated, in which year of eligibility was Larry Little voted into the Hall of Fame?

    a. 7th

    b. 8th

    c. 9th

    d. 10th

11. What ended Dwight Stephenson's ironman streak of 107 consecutive games played for the Dolphins?

    a. Player's strike

    b. Knee injury

    c. Birth of his child

    d. Rested before playoffs

12. Whose injury in 1981 opened the spot for Dwight Stephenson to earn his first career start?

    a. Bob DeMarco

    b. Bob Kuechenberg

c. Jim Langer

d. Mark Dennard

13. What injury forced Nick Buoniconti to miss the entire 1975 season?

    a. Shoulder

    b. Foot

    c. Knee

    d. Thumb

14. Buoniconti hosted *Inside the NFL* until it moved from HBO to Showtime.

    a. True

    b. False

15. Which NFL career record did Dan Marino not hold after he retired in 1999?

    a. Most regular-season passing attempts

    b. Most regular-season passing yards

    c. Most playoff passing attempts

    d. Most regular-season completions

16. Dan Marino was the last of the three Hall of Fame quarterbacks from the 1983 draft class to be inducted.

    a. True

    b. False

17. When was the first year Jason Taylor was voted into the Pro Bowl?

    a. 2000

    b. 2001

c. 2002

d. 2003

18. Which future Hall-of-Famer was not a teammate of Jason Taylor's on the Dolphins?

    a. Cris Carter

    b. Thurman Thomas

    c. Junior Seau

    d. Troy Vincent

19. How many seasons was Don Shula the head coach of the Dolphins?

    a. 25

    b. 26

    c. 27

    d. 28

20. How many of the Dolphins Hall-of-Famers did Don Shula coach during his tenure in Miami?

    a. 6

    b. 7

    c. 8

    d. 9

QUIZ ANSWERS

1. B – 1987

2. A – 1

3. C – Linebacker

4. A – True

5. D – 12

6. C – 21

7. B – 63 percent

8. A – True

9. C – $750

10. B – 8th

11. A – Player's strike

12. D – Mark Dennard

13. D – Thumb

14. B – False

15. C – Most playoff passing attempts

16. A – True

17. A – 2000

18. D – Troy Vincent

19. B – 26

20. C – 8

DID YOU KNOW?

1. Paul Warfield's football career began in Canton at Fawcett Stadium. The Ohio native wasn't sure football was right for him after he sustained numerous bruises in his first high school game for Warren Harding High School. But that same season, Warfield played in Canton's famous stadium and played well enough that the bumps and bruises of the game didn't matter and he fell in love with football. It took a quarter-century after that game for Warfield to get his name enshrined in the Pro Football Hall of Fame in 1983, becoming the first former Dolphins player to earn the honor.

2. Don Shula pointed out an amazing fact about Jim Langer when he was presenting him for induction into the Hall of Fame in 1987. The coach said Langer only needed help on three of his more than 500 blocking assignments during the 1972 season. Shula said it was a testament to the leader Langer was for the offensive line and a major reason why the Dolphins were able to run the ball so well during the 1970s with their stable of running backs.

3. Larry Csonka was at the dedication for the Hall of Fame when it was opened in 1963 in Canton. He and some friends drove down from Stow, Ohio to see Bronko Nagurski, whose career Csonka said he hoped he shadowed. Of course, the 15-year-old and friends didn't

have the money to park near the building and they had to slip under some ropes and avoid ushers, but he wound up being 10 feet away from his hero. It only took 24 years for Csonka to earn his bust alongside Nagurski's in Canton, and Csonka said he tries to visit the Hall of Fame annually.

4. Bob Griese spent a minute or two of his 1990 Hall of Fame speech talking about his disagreements with Shula. The biggest one, he said, was when he would have to wipe down his glasses between plays due to the condensation buildup on the lenses. Shula would be panicking on the sideline telling his quarterback to hurry up but Griese said he knew how much time was left on the play clock at all times. This part of his speech is probably most memorable, though, for Griese pulling out a pair of sunglasses with windshield wipers on them as a joke for what he would have used if the rain got too bad for him to see on the field.

5. Don Shula presented five of his Dolphins players for enshrinement into the Hall of Fame (Csonka, Griese, Langer, Little, and Dwight Stephenson), but he was presented for induction in 1997 by his son, Dave. During his presentation, Dave Shula relayed two stories about his father's early time in the game. Don Shula forged his parents' signature to start playing football after his mother told him he couldn't play in the eighth grade and he persuaded his entire team to keep the secret for him. Later, his Detroit Lions defense allowed a 60-yard touchdown on the first play of his first game as Detroit's defensive coordinator. Shula has 15 former players enshrined in

Canton, fourth most in NFL history behind George Halas, Vince Lombardi, and Paul Brown.

6. Stephenson made quite the first impression on Shula during his first scrimmage with the Dolphins. Miami had just drafted the center out of Alabama and Miami's offense was running a screen pass in the scrimmage. Stephenson was doing his duty on the play and flattened the cornerback, Don McNeal, who had been Stephenson's teammate at Alabama. At that point, Shula said, he realized that the opposing teams were in trouble because Stephenson was going to do that consistently in games for the Dolphins.

7. Many assumed that Nick Buoniconti would be too small to play professional football. As he recounted during his induction remarks, his coach at Notre Dame told teams, "if you tell Nick to run through a brick wall, he'll run through the wall, but he'll leave a small hole." Despite being an All-American linebacker at Notre Dame, Buoniconti was overlooked in the NFL draft and lasted until the 13th round of the AFL Draft. Buoniconti got the last laugh, though, as he was inducted into the Hall of Fame in 2001 because he played bigger than his 5-foot-11 frame.

8. Dan Marino admitted during his Hall of Fame speech how nervous he was for his first start in 1983 against Buffalo. He recounted that, as he was standing on the sidelines waiting to head out on the field, Lyle Blackwood came up to Marino with a calm look on his face and shook his hand. All Blackwood told him during that handshake was "Dan,

good luck today. And I don't want you to feel any pressure but remember this one thing: If you play bad, we'll lose." Marino threw for 322 yards and three touchdowns, but the Dolphins lost 38-35 in overtime to the Bills that day.

9. Jason Taylor worked most days after school to help his single mother make ends meet. One day, the coach at the local high school pulled over when Taylor was working in a neighbor's yard and asked him if he had any interest in playing football. That decision at 16 years old led the University of Akron to take a chance on Taylor, an undersized player without a solid position group, by giving him a scholarship. Taylor, though, almost quit five days into his first training camp because of how hard Jimmy Johnson was coaching the team but a little call from mom refocused him and kept him in Miami.

10. In addition to 10 Hall-of-Famers who played most of their careers with the Dolphins, six others have ties to the franchise. Cris Carter and Thurman Thomas both played one season for Miami near the end of their careers and Junior Seau played three seasons for the Dolphins from 2003-05. Miami also had three coaches or executives enshrined in Canton: Bobby Beathard was enshrined in 2018 and served as Miami's director of player personnel from 1972-78, Jimmy Johnson, who coached the Dolphins from 1996 to 1999, was scheduled to be inducted honor in 2020 along with Miami's former director of pro scouting George Young, who was with the franchise from 1975 to 1978.

CHAPTER 10:

DRAFT DAY

QUIZ TIME!

1. Who was the first draft pick in Miami Dolphins history?

    a. Bob Griese

    b. Frank Emmanuel

    c. Rick Norton

    d. Jim Grabowski

2. In which round of the 1970 NFL draft did the Dolphins select Jake Scott out of Georgia?

    a. 5th

    b. 6th

    c. 7th

    d. 8th

3. Which future Super Bowl champion quarterback did the Dolphins draft in the 1970s, although he never played for the team?

    a. Doug Williams

    b. Joe Theismann

c. Danny White

d. Ron Jaworski

4. On which impact player did the Dolphins use a ninth-round pick in the 1971 NFL draft?

   a. Tim Foley

   b. Vern Den Herder

   c. Curtis Johnson

   d. Ed Newman

5. Which of Dan Marino's favorite targets was selected in the same 1983 draft class as he was?

   a. Mark Duper

   b. Tony Nathan

   c. Mark Clayton

   d. Dan Johnson

6. All five of the Hall-of-Famers the Dolphins drafted spent most of their career in Miami.

   a. True

   b. False

7. Which pick did the Dolphins use to select O.J. McDuffie in the first round of the 1993 draft?

   a. 19

   b. 21

   c. 23

   d. 25

8. Who is NOT one of the players the Dolphins picked ahead of Zach Thomas in the 1996 NFL draft before selecting him in the fifth round?

a. Shane Burton

b. Jerris McPhail

c. Kirk Pointer

d. Jeff Buckey

9. Which of these players was not a top-10 pick by the Dolphins?

   a. Minkah Fitzpatrick

   b. Troy Vincent

   c. Richmond Webb

   d. Ted Ginn Jr.

10. Bob Griese was the last top-five pick the Dolphins had until drafting Jake Long at No. 1 overall.

    a. True

    b. False

11. The 1997 draft was generous to the Dolphins because they drafted Sam Madison and Jason Taylor that year. However, neither one of them was a first-round pick; who did Miami take with the 15th pick that year?

    a. Billy Milner

    b. John Avery

    c. Yatil Greene

    d. Daryl Gardener

12. Miami's first two picks in the 2001 NFL draft hailed from which Big Ten school?

    a. Michigan

    b. Penn State

c. Ohio State

d. Wisconsin

13. Miami drafted John Beck and Chad Henne in the second round of consecutive drafts.

a. True

b. False

14. Widely considered the biggest draft bust in Dolphins history, Dion Jordan was the third overall pick in what year?

a. 2013

b. 2014

c. 2012

d. 2015

15. When was the last time the Dolphins did not draft in the first round?

a. 2001

b. 2002

c. 2003

d. 2004

16. From which team did Miami draft Norm Evans in the 1966 expansion draft?

a. San Diego Chargers

b. Houston Oilers

c. Oakland Raiders

d. New York Jets

17. The Dolphins have picked more quarterbacks than wide receivers in the first round.

    a. True
    b. False

18. What is not a position the Dolphins have used at least 100 draft picks on in their history?

    a. Offensive line
    b. Defensive line
    c. Defensive backs
    d. Running backs

19. How many kickers and punters has Miami drafted?

    a. 29
    b. 24
    c. 17
    d. 13

20. Who is the only long snapper ever drafted by the Dolphins?

    a. Ethan Albright
    b. John Denney
    c. Blake Ferguson
    d. Matt Orzech

QUIZ ANSWERS

1. D – Jim Grabowski

2. C – 7th

3. B – Joe Theismann

4. B – Vern Den Herder

5. C – Mark Clayton

6. A – True

7. D – 25

8. D – Jeff Buckey

9. A – Minkah Fitzpatrick

10. B – False

11. C – Yatil Greene

12. D – Wisconsin

13. A – True

14. A -- 2013

15. C – 2003

16. B – Houston Oilers

17. B – False

18. D – Running Backs

19. D – 13

20. C – Blake Ferguson

DID YOU KNOW?

1. The Dolphins drafted Joe Theismann with the 99th overall pick in 1971 but the star quarterback never signed with Miami. He and Joe Robbie had agreed upon a contract but Theismann, acting as his own agent, didn't like the fact that the signing bonus would be paid out over three years and he would forfeit some of that money if he was forced to miss the season because of the Vietnam War draft. Instead, he signed a deal with the Toronto Argonauts and played in Canada for three seasons until Washington traded for his rights.

2. Much is made about the 1983 NFL draft that produced seven Hall-of-Famers in the first round, including three quarterbacks. Dan Marino was the last of the six quarterbacks selected that season, dropping all the way to Miami with the 27th pick. The slide was frustrating for Marino, who some may argue was the best of the bunch that season but he said his father put it all in perspective for him once the Dolphins selected him. The elder Marino told his frustrated son, "It doesn't really matter where you go, if you're good at what you, you're going to be successful either way."

3. Mark Clayton might go down as one of the biggest steals in Dolphins history as an eighth-round pick in that 1983 draft. No receiver drafted by Miami has caught more

touchdowns or had more receiving yards in his NFL career than Clayton, who did most of that while playing for the Dolphins. He remembers the Dolphins showing interest in him when scout Elbert Dubenion came to Louisville to watch him practice, but he said he didn't believe the interest was real because every other team who had come to scout him had said similar things.

4. John Offerdahl almost made a costly error during the 1986 NFL draft. The linebacker was being profiled for a *Sports Illustrated* story and he was watching ESPN when Bill Walsh called to let him know the 49ers were going to draft him. So Offerdahl disconnected his phone and celebrated until ESPN caught up to the draft order almost an hour later and announced that San Francisco had traded the pick. A few seconds after Offerdahl reconnected the phone, Don Shula called him to let him know Miami was going to draft him with the 52nd pick.

5. O.J. McDuffie fell asleep for most of the draft selection before his being chosen with the 25th overall pick in 1993. McDuffie had been at Penn State's spring game the night before the draft and he had road-tripped back to his mom's house in Cleveland the morning of the draft. He was so tired that he fell asleep watching the draft and woke up around the 19th pick. He received only one phone call throughout the entire draft process, which came from Don Shula after Miami drafted him. McDuffie called that conversation "the best phone call of my life."

6. Zach Thomas is one of the many late-round gems the Dolphins discovered in the draft over the years. Thomas was a fifth-round pick who failed miserably at the NFL Combine after being a Butkus Award finalist as the best linebacker in college football. Miami sent its special teams coordinator, Mike Westhoff, to scout Thomas because, at the very least, Jimmy Johnson thought Thomas could be a good special teams player. Westhoff really liked Thomas so he fudged some numbers in order to sell him to Johnson and the rest, as they say, is history.

7. Jason Taylor found his way onto Miami's draft board thanks to Washington head coach Norv Turner, who coached Taylor in the Senior Bowl. Washington was scared off by Taylor's size, so Turner told Jimmy Johnson about the linebacker from Akron. The only problem is that Johnson wanted both cornerback Sam Madison and Taylor when the Dolphins pick was up in the second round. Assuming – correctly as well – that Taylor would still be there in the third round and knowing Madison was highly coveted by other teams, the Dolphins drafted Madison in the second round and Taylor in the third.

8. Jarvis Landry suffered the crushing feeling of not being a first-round pick in a packed ballroom in Baton Rouge, Louisiana. The LSU product threw a giant party for friends and family for the first round of the 2014 draft but he was not selected, and he ended up in his hotel room that night in tears. "I (was) just heartbroken," Landry said years later, reflecting on that day. "I felt like I didn't achieve my goal. I

felt like I let my family down. I didn't know what Day 2 would be. I didn't know what Day 3 would be. I didn't know if I'd get drafted." The Dolphins drafted Landry in the second round with the 63rd pick, giving him a spot to begin his professional football career.

9. The Dolphins had three first-round picks in the 2020 NFL draft. The third one could have played out much differently if not for New Orleans. The Saints drafted Michigan offensive lineman Cesar Ruiz with the 24th pick, based on intel that Miami thought very highly of the center. The Dolphins traded down from No. 26 to No. 30 and drafted Auburn cornerback Noah Igbinoghene. Had Ruiz not been drafted, Miami might have bolstered its offensive line a bit more and changed the direction of its second-round selection.

10. Patrick Surtain II, the son of former Dolphins cornerback Patrick Surtain, is already drawing hype as a potential first-round pick in the 2021 NFL draft. If he were to be selected in the first round, he would become at least the eighth son of a former Dolphins player to become a first-round pick. Among the first seven are brothers Nick and Joey Bosa (John Bosa played for Miami from 1987-89) and Tremaine and Terrell Edmunds, whose father Ferrell Edmunds was a tight end for the Dolphins from 1988-92. The other picks are cornerback Marlon Humphrey, running back Mark Ingram Jr., and wide receiver Breshad Perriman.

CHAPTER 11:

LET'S MAKE A DEAL

QUIZ TIME!

1. Who was not part of the deal when Miami acquired Nick Buoniconti from the Patriots in 1969?

   a. John Stofa
   b. John Bramlett
   c. Kim Hammond
   d. 1970 5th-round pick

2. Which cornerback did the Dolphins send to the Chargers in 1969 for Larry Little?

   a. Bob Petrella
   b. Jimmy Warren
   c. Mack Lamb
   d. Dick Washington

3. Who did the Dolphins acquire in exchange for their 1971 first-round pick?

   a. Paul Warfield
   b. Don Shula

    c. Manny Fernandez

    d. Bob DeMarco

4. What did the Dolphins eventually receive from Washington in exchange for the rights to Joe Theismann in 1974?

    a. 1975 1st-round pick

    b. 1975 2nd-round pick

    c. 1976 1st-round pick

    d. 1976 2nd-round pick

5. Which safety did Miami receive when it traded Jake Scott to Washington in 1977?

    a. Bryant Salter

    b. Charlie Babb

    c. Vern Roberson

    d. Rick Volk

6. The third-round pick Miami acquired in the Randy Crowder trade with Tampa Bay was used to select Tony Nathan.

    a. True

    b. False

7. Who did Miami trade to Minnesota in 1980 in exchange for fifth- and sixth-round picks?

    a. Tim Foley

    b. Mike Current

    c. Larry Csonka

    d. Jim Langer

8. In which of these seasons did the Dolphins make a trade?

   a. 1988

   b. 1982

   c. 1986

   d. 1985

9. The Dolphins made a selection with the draft pick they acquired from Pittsburgh in exchange for David Woodley.

   a. True

   b. False

10. How many games did Randal Hill play for the Dolphins before being shipped off to the Cardinals in 1991?

    a. 3

    b. 2

    c. 1

    d. 0

11. The first-round pick the Dolphins acquired IN the Randal Hill trade was used to draft Troy Vincent.

    a. True

    b. False

12. What draft picks did Miami send New England to acquire Irving Fryar in 1993?

    a. 1993 3rd and 1994 2nd

    b. 1993 2nd and 1993 3rd

    c. 1994 2nd and 1994 3rd

    d. 1993 2nd and 1994 3rd

13. Who did Green Bay send to Miami in 1995 to complete the future considerations clause in a previous deal?

    a. DeWayne Dotson
    b. Terrell Buckley
    c. Calvin Jackson
    d. Gary Clark

14. What draft pick was not involved in the trade for Ricky Williams?

    a. 2002 1st-round
    b. 2003 1st-round
    c. 2003 2nd-round
    d. 2002 4th-round

15. What draft pick did the Dolphins surrender in the trade with San Diego for Junior Seau?

    a. 2004 2nd-round
    b. 2004 3rd-round
    c. 2004 4th-round
    d. 2004 5th-round

16. Which quarterback was not part of a Dolphins trade during the 2005 or 2006 seasons?

    a. Sage Rosenfels
    b. Joey Harrington
    c. Cleo Lemon
    d. A.J. Feeley

17. Which player did the Dolphins not draft with a selection for which they traded?

a. Chad Henne

b. Randy McMichael

c. John Beck

d. Jarvis Landry

18. In Miami's two trades involving Brandon Marshall, the Dolphins sent a first-round pick to Denver and received one from Chicago.

a. True

b. False

19. Which player did Miami trade away in exchange for the fifth-round pick it used to draft Jay Ajayi?

a. Dannell Ellerbe

b. Davone Bess

c. Jonathan Martin

d. Mike Wallace

20. Which player did the Dolphins not trade right before the 2019 season began?

a. Minkah Fitzpatrick

b. Laremy Tunsil

c. Kiko Alonso

d. Kenny Stills

QUIZ ANSWERS

1. A – John Stofa

2. C – Mack Lamb

3. B – Don Shula

4. C – 1976 1st-round pick

5. A – Bryant Salter

6. A – True

7. D – Jim Langer

8. D -- 1985

9. B – False

10. C – 1

11. A – True

12. D – 1993 2nd & 1994 3rd

13. B – Terrell Buckley

14. C – 2003 2nd-round

15. D – 2004 5th-round

16. A – Sage Rosenfels

17. B – John Beck

18. B – False

19. D – Mike Wallace

20. A – Minkah Fitzpatrick

DID YOU KNOW?

1. Larry Little's eating habits led to his being traded to Miami in 1968. The Chargers, who had spent $750 on Little as an undrafted free agent, were getting increasingly frustrated at Little's growing size as his weight neared 300 pounds. His penchant for eating two half chickens per day earned him the nickname "Chicken Little." Though he played in every game for the Chargers that first season, the eating became enough of a problem that San Diego offloaded him to Miami, where he got his weight in check and became a Hall-of-Famer.

2. Miami was on the receiving end of the most controversial trade in Browns' history when Cleveland sent Paul Warfield to Miami for a first-round pick. The Browns used that pick on quarterback Mike Phipps out of Purdue, who flamed out with Cleveland while Warfield solidified his Hall of Fame credentials with the Dolphins. Browns owner Art Modell said at the time, "Paul has played so well for us and is such a high type person that I hated like the devil to consider any trade involving him. However, it was the overwhelming consensus of all our combined thinking that we had a pressing need for backup protection behind quarterback Bill Nelsen."

3. Jimmy Johnson earned the nickname "Trader Jimmy" for his 51 trades in five years in Dallas. He didn't make that

many moves with the Dolphins, but he still was very active in the trade market during his time with the Miami. He made seven trades in four seasons with the Dolphins that involved a player in addition to numerous other draft-day deals.

4. Miami sent a second-round pick to Minnesota in 2006 for Daunte Culpepper because of Drew Brees' shoulder. Brees visited Miami as a free agent after the 2005 season as he was coming off surgery for a torn labrum and rotator cuff. The Dolphins, after giving him an extensive physical exam, weren't sold on the idea that Brees was going to recover in time for the 2006 season or that his shoulder wasn't compromised. So, they balked on the future Hall-of-Famer and sent a draft pick to the Vikings for Culpepper, who was seen as less likely to re-injure himself after tearing multiple knee ligaments the previous season.

5. The Patriots had a chance to sign Wes Welker to an expensive offer sheet as a restricted free agent that Miami had no chance to match and would only have to surrender a second-round pick. But in a rare sign of respect with a divisional rival, the Patriots ended up working out a trade with Miami for second- and seventh-round picks in exchange for Welker. It was a bad trade for Miami in hindsight because Welker shredded the AFC East as one of Tom Brady's best receivers, but it could have been far worse for the Dolphins if they had just let Welker walk.

6. Miami's decision to trade Brandon Marshall in 2012 was a

shock to many after Marshall's success in his two seasons with the Dolphins. The rumors at the time were that Miami made the trade to free cap space to sign Peyton Manning, but the team denied that rumor, and Manning didn't end up signing with the team. However, Marshall said the trade was a career-saving move that worked out well for him. He said he felt more supported after being reunited with Jay Cutler in Chicago and understood why the Dolphins had to make the move. He said he knew it didn't make sense for Miami financially to pay Marshall the money he was owed in an offense that wasn't going to let him flourish.

7. HBO's *Hard Knocks* gave fans an inside look at trade negotiations as the Dolphins were set to trade Vontae Davis to the Colts in 2012. The behind-the-scenes television show followed general manager Jeff Ireland as he worked the phones with Indianapolis to garner the best deal possible. The Colts initiated the conversations and offered a fifth and a sixth to Miami for Davis. That quickly improved to a third and a sixth, but Ireland was still not satisfied and reminded Indianapolis that they had called him. The deal eventually settled on a second-round pick and a conditional sixth-rounder for the troubled cornerback.

8. There are many reasons that a player might be traded away from a team; sometimes it's a personal reason and sometimes it's a football reason. In Jay Ajayi's case, it seems that the Dolphins were unhappy with his impact on the culture in the locker room. After Miami shipped its star

running back to Philadelphia in the middle of the 2017 season, reports started to circulate that Ajayi didn't have the required buy-in and was complaining about his lack of touches, even after wins.

9. In a similar fashion, Miami felt the need to trade Jarvis Landry the following year due to attitude issues. However, Landry was very public with his side of the story after the Dolphins completed the trade to send him to the Browns. In an interview with ESPN after the trade, Landry admitted that his strained relationship with head coach Adam Gase was a reason why he was likely traded, but that he felt like it didn't work because the two were similarly competitive people. He said Gase's running joke for players in his doghouse was that he was going to trade them to Cleveland. So, in some respects, it made sense that Landy believed, "I just felt like, for some reason, Adam sent me here to die."

10. The Dolphins have had the foresight to trade up in the draft for a pair of stars in their history. In 1998, Miami sent its first-round pick in the 2000 draft to Carolina for a second-round pick to select Patrick Surtain. Three years later, the Dolphins traded up four spots in the second round with Dallas to draft Chris Chambers. Both players were among the best draft picks in Dolphins history and they became key members of Miami's teams in the early 2000s.

CHAPTER 12:

WRITING THE RECORD BOOK

QUIZ TIME!

1. Which player played the most seasons for the Dolphins?

    a. Dan Marino

    b. Jason Taylor

    c. Bob Kuechenberg

    d. Bob Griese

2. Who holds the Dolphins record for most consecutive games played at 224?

    a. Jason Taylor

    b. Jim Langer

    c. Bob Kuechenberg

    d. John Denney

3. Who holds the Dolphins record for most consecutive Pro Bowl appearances with seven?

    a. Richmond Webb

    b. Dan Marino

    c. Chris Chambers

    d. Jim Langer

4. Only one player has ever scored 1,000 career points for the Dolphins.

   a. True

   b. False

5. In which season did Olindo Mare set the Dolphins scoring record with 144 points on 39 field goals and 27 extra points?

   a. 1997

   b. 1999

   c. 2001

   d. 2003

6. Olindo Mare still holds the record for most field goals in a game with7.

   a. True

   b. False

7. Who holds the Dolphins record for most touchdowns scored in his Miami career?

   a. Larry Csonka

   b. McDuffie

   c. Nat Moore

   d. Mark Clayton

8. In 1984, Mark Clayton set the Dolphins single-season touchdown record when he hauled in how many touchdown passes?

   a. 16

   b. 17

c. 18

d. 19

9. Who is the Dolphins' all-time leading rusher?

    a. Ronnie Brown

    b. Ricky Williams

    c. Larry Csonka

    d. Mercury Morris

10. How many yards did Ricky Williams rush for when he set the single-season rushing record in 2002?

    a. 1,708

    b. 1,789

    c. 1,853

    d. 1,901

11. In consecutive weeks during the 2002 season, Ricky Williams set the top-two single-game rushing totals in Dolphins history.

    a. True

    b. False

12. How long is the longest non-scoring run in Dolphins history?

    a. 60 yards

    b. 65 yards

    c. 70 yards

    d. 75 yards

13. Who was Miami playing when Dan Marino set the franchise record with 521 passing yards?

a. New England Patriots

b. Buffalo Bills

c. Indianapolis Colts

d. New York Jets

14. How many consecutive games did Dan Marino throw a touchdown pass to set the franchise record?

a. 27

b. 30

c. 33

d. 36

15. Who holds the Miami record for most consecutive games with a reception?

a. Jarvis Landry

b. McDuffie

c. Mark Clayton

d. Chris Chambers

16. Who holds the Dolphin record for total yards from scrimmage in a career?

a. Mark Clayton

b. Mark Duper

c. Ricky Williams

d. Larry Csonka

17. The Dolphin offense in 1984 might have been the most prolific in the team's history. Which of these single-season records does the team not currently hold?

a. Most points

b. Most passing attempts

c. Most net yards

d. Most touchdowns

18. Jason Taylor is the only Dolphins player to register 100 career sacks with the franchise.

a. True

b. False

19. Who holds the Dolphins record for most career takeaways?

a. Dick Anderson

b. Sam Madison

c. Jake Scott

d. Jason Taylor

20. How long was the longest punt in Dolphin history?

a. 73 yards

b. 74 yards

c. 76 yards

d. 77 yards

QUIZ ANSWERS

1. A – Dan Marino

2. D – John Denney

3. A – Richmond Webb

4. A – True

5. B – 1999

6. B – False

7. D – Mark Clayton

8. C – 18

9. C – Larry Csonka

10. C – 1,853

11. A – True

12. C – 70 yards

13. D – New York Jets

14. B – 30

15. C – Mark Clayton

16. B – Mark Duper

17. B – Most passing attempts

18. A – True

19. A – Dick Anderson

20. D – 77 yards

DID YOU KNOW?

1. The Dolphins are proof that perhaps the cold weather does affect teams from warmer weather. Miami is 3-7 in the 10 coldest games in franchise history, though the Dolphins did beat Kansas City 38-31 on December 21, 2008, in the coldest game they ever played; it was 10 degrees Fahrenheit in Kansas City. The coldest game in Miami was on Christmas Eve 1989 when the Chiefs beat the Dolphins 27-24 in 40-degree weather. On the other side of the coin, Miami has won six of the seven warmest games in franchise history, including a 38-10 win in Arizona in 1996 in the only game Miami has ever played in 100-degree weather. The previous year, the Dolphins beat the Jets in the warmest home game in franchise history at 94 degrees.

2. Miami has a winning record in every month of the year except January, during which the Dolphins are 5-6 in their history. The Dolphins are 122-102 in November for the most wins in any month in franchise history, but that is also the worst winning percentage of the four main months of the season. Miami has a .558 winning percentage in October (118-93-3), a .556 winning percentage in December (114-91), and a .553 winning percentage in August/September (98-79-1).

3. Despite New England's recent success, the Dolphins still hold a slight 56-53 edge over the Patriots in the all-time

series because it has split the season series six times in seven seasons between 2013 and 2019. Miami is 61-50-1 all-time against the Buffalo Bills, including winning all 20 games the teams played in the 1970s. The only divisional rival with a winning record against Miami is the Jets, who hold a narrow 55-53-1 advantage in the series, even though Miami has won six of the last eight games with New York.

4. Miami's single-game scoring record came in a blowout 55-14 win over the St. Louis Cardinals in 1977. That game featured Bob Griese setting the Dolphins record with six touchdown passes – later tied by Dan Marino in 1986 – with three of those passes going to Nat Moore. Miami also ran for two touchdowns to set the franchise record with eight touchdowns scored in the game. The Dolphins also set the record for most first downs in a game with 34, though the record was broken in 2014.

5. The most decisive win in Dolphins history came during that perfect 1972 season when Miami stomped New England 52-0 for one of the 26 shutouts in franchise history. It was Don Shula's 100th win as a head coach and set the record for most extra points made in a game with 7, which was tied in the 1977 St. Louis game.

6. The Patriots were also the victim for the largest comeback in franchise history as Miami rallied from a 24-0 deficit in the second quarter to upend the Patriots in the 1974 regular-season finale. The Dolphins did most of the

rallying in that second quarter as they scored 17 straight points to cut the deficit to 24-17 at halftime. Earl Morrall threw for two touchdowns and Don Nottingham ran for two more, including the eventual game-winning two-yard plunge in the fourth quarter.

7. On New Year's Day 2012 against the Jets, the Dolphins embarked on the longest drive in franchise history. The 21-play possession took up 12 minutes and 29 seconds of game time while covering 94 yards. The drive spanned the third and fourth quarters and featured 13 passing plays and eight rushing plays, capped off by a 1-yard touchdown toss from Matt Moore to Charles Clay to give Miami its first lead of the game. The Dolphins won the game 19-17.

8. The longest play in Dolphins history was Mercury Morris' 105-yard kickoff return touchdown against Cincinnati in 1969. It is the longest of the five 100-plus-yard kickoff returns in team history, though Morris is the only player to only have one such return in his career. Ted Ginn Jr. and Jakeem Grant Sr. both had multiple 100-plus-yard kickoff return touchdowns in their careers with Miami. Ginn even did it in the same game with a 100-yard and 101-yard return against the Jets in 2009.

9. The 1999 Dolphins snuck into the playoffs at 9-7 and went on the road to upset the Seattle Seahawks in the wild card round. Yet it was their divisional round game against the Jaguars that has that team in Miami's record book for the

wrong reason. That 62-7 loss to Jacksonville was the most decisive loss in Dolphins history and the most points allowed in team history as well. The Jaguars' 8 touchdowns tied the record for the most allowed in a single game and the 24 first-quarter points allowed tied a record. Miami didn't pick up any first downs on the ground and tied the record with 5 lost fumbles in the game. Fred Taylor busted out a 90-yard touchdown run to set the record for the longest running play against the Dolphins in team history.

10. Tom Brady has been a thorn in Miami's side for as long as he's been the starting quarterback in New England. He holds most of the opponent passing records against the Dolphins, both in a career and a single game. He leads in career passing yards (8,185), single-game passing yards (517), career touchdown passes (67), single-game touchdown passes (6), and the most 300-yard passing games (8). He and Wes Welker even connected on the longest pass against Miami in team history, a 99-yard completion in 2011.

CONCLUSION

By this point, we hope you're filled to the brim with new facts about your favorite NFL team, the Miami Dolphins. Whether it's new information about some of Miami's franchise records or learning some behind-the-scenes knowledge about your favorite players and moments, we hope you enjoyed this trip through the rich history of the Dolphins. We did our best to cover it all, from the dominance of the 1970s through the leaner times in recent years.

The Miami Dolphins have a rich tapestry of history with legendary coach Don Shula and the tremendous success he had in 26 years in Miami. It is no surprise that the Dolphins have had their share of struggles since Shula's retirement but they seem to be on the right track moving forward into the 2020s and beyond. The Dolphins are still the only team to go through a season unblemished, and their dominance in the 1970s probably could have produced more Hall-of-Famers than they have right now. The two Super Bowl championships might not be enough to prove their success but five Super Bowl appearances in 13 seasons is nothing to be ashamed about.

We designed this book for you, the fan, to be able to embrace your favorite team and feel closer to them. Maybe you weren't familiar with the history of the franchise and their few years toiling in the AFL before the merger. Perhaps you didn't realize how fortunate Miami was to sign the right free agents at the right time. There's also the possibility we couldn't stump you at all and you're the ultimate superfan. No matter how well you did on the quizzes, we hope we captured the spirit of the Dolphins and injected you with even more pride for your team.

The Dolphins believe they have their quarterback of the future in Tua Tagovailoa and they have made some big free agent signings to help shore up the defense. There is hope again that the Dolphins will be contenders in the AFC East and a threat to return to the Super Bowl in the near future. But that's the great thing about being a fan: Hope springs eternal every year when the records are reset and everyone still has to prove it on the field. Maybe the Dolphins will be able to do just that and rebuild themselves into a perennial playoff contender under Brian Flores with so much young talent on both sides of the ball.

Printed in Great Britain
by Amazon

13075656R00078